GOD'S POSITIVE KINGDOM

# God's Positive Kingdom

STEPHEN GAUKROGER

KINGSWAY PUBLICATIONS

EASTBOURNE

Biblical quotations are from the
New International Version © 1973, 1978, 1984 by the
International Bible Society. Anglicisation
© 1979, 1984 by Hodder & Stoughton

*Front cover photo: Tony Stone Photolibrary – London*

**British Library Cataloguing in Publication Data**

Gaukroger, Stephen *1954–*
God's Positive Kingdom.
1. Bible. Special subjects. Christian doctrine. Kingdom of
God
I. Title
236

ISBN 0-86065-893-7

Printed in Great Britain for
KINGSWAY PUBLICATIONS LTD
1 St Anne's Road, Eastbourne, E Sussex BN21 3UN by
Richard Clay Ltd, Bungay, Suffolk
Typeset by Watermark, Norfolk House, Cromer, Norfolk

# Contents

# 1

## God's Positive Kingdom

For Christians, the kingdom of God is crucial. We are part of that kingdom and we are working for its coming over the whole earth. But before we can take the kingdom into the world, we need to understand something about what is wrong with the world; we must be able to recognise the nature of the opposition.

Dear friends, do not believe every spirit, but test the spirits to see whether they are from God, because many false prophets have gone out into the world. This is how you can recognise the Spirit of God: every spirit that acknowledges that Jesus Christ has come in the flesh is from God, but every spirit that does not acknowledge Jesus is not from God. This is the spirit of the antichrist, which you have heard is coming and even now is already in the world.

You, dear children, are from God and have overcome them, because the one who is in you is greater than the one who is in the world. They are from the world and therefore speak from the viewpoint of the world, and the world listens to them. We are from God, and whoever knows God listens to us; but whoever is not from God does not listen to us. This is how we recognise the Spirit of truth and the spirit of falsehood (1 Jn 4:1–6).

When the Fall occurred, something irreversible happened to humanity – irreversible, that is, by anyone but Jesus. The effects were catastrophic and universal. Adam and Eve fell, leaving humanity down the ages with the legacy of their rebellion.

What happened was that a man and a woman, our ancestors, lived in perfect harmony with God. He gave them a command not to eat the fruit from a particular tree (it wasn't an apple, despite all the rumours, just a fruit). But Eve was tempted by the Serpent. 'Did God really say you must not eat from any tree in the garden?' he asked her. Eve mumbled something about not quite being able to remember, took the fruit and ate it, and so did Adam. In an instant they both realised that they were naked. They were ashamed to face God and tried to hide from him in the garden.

The Fall was threefold. First, mankind fell away from God's ideal pattern of living. Secondly, creation fell: weeds grew for the first time, earthquakes, volcanoes and other natural disasters occurred, so that 'the whole creation has been groaning as in the pains of childbirth right up to the present time' (Rom 8:22). Thirdly, the whole way we perceive life, our philosophy and our culture, fell. So we find ourselves in a world where Satan is 'ruler of the kingdom of the air' (Eph 2:2).

Of course, God reigns supreme in the entire universe. He is the Lord of our world and will one day displace Satan. But meanwhile, in this small kingdom called planet Earth, a usurper is on the throne: Satan has dominated the creation, and also the thinking and culture of mankind ever since the Fall. That is why we are bent and twisted until we turn to Jesus; that is why we need the fruit of the crucifixion and resurrection to straighten us out again. And it is at that point, when we have made Jesus Lord of our lives instead of Satan, that we become God's rebel soldiers in a land dominated by a false prince. In the days of Robin Hood and his Merry Men, Prince John was on the throne while the rightful King Richard was away at the Crusades. It's a little like that for us. Prince Satan is on the throne and we are outlaws, constantly subject to satanic attack as we attempt to uphold the values of the King who is coming.

## The power of the negative

So we live in Satan's negative kingdom, and that negative outlook pervades the whole of human society. In fact, it can be so powerful that we sometimes bring it into church with us – which is just what Satan wants.

If you put one rotten apple in the fruit bowl with several sound ones, it doesn't improve. Instead, all the good apples become rotten – the negative wins. What kind of day have you had? A thousand things may happen to you in any day. How many bad things need to happen to make your day a bad one? Two, three, four? Just four negative things out of a thousand are enough to dominate your life and spoil your day. The negative outweighs the positive.

Satan causes this world to focus on the negative. The news broadcasts are hardly ever good. They focus on the things that are wrong, the disasters and tragedies, not the things that are right.

Would you like to know one way of getting a crowd to come to church? Go out into your town centre and shoot someone. You'll have a crowd in seconds! Whether it's a car crash or a fire, any accident pulls a crowd immediately. But getting that crowd into church, where the good news is, can be close to impossible. The negative kingdom of Satan dominates our entire world.

You can check this. Look back on your day, your week, your newspaper, the TV – everything in your life that happens without God's input. The negative wins.

## Satan's negative kingdom

God is the author of everything positive; Satan is the author of nothing but negative. He is a cheat as well as a liar, because he has never had a single original idea: all his vices are twisted versions of God's virtues.

Take lust and inordinate sexual desire. Satan didn't invent sex, he invented the cheapening and twisting of it. God created the good gift of sex, but because Satan has no creative power of his own, all he can do is warp and distort it because he is opposed to God's positive creation.

As Christians we are part of God's positive kingdom, and that makes us a prime target. Satan wants to infiltrate our lives in the most negative and destructive ways. He wants to worm his way right inside the church, and he finds one easy route – through the tongue.

Right back in Eden, Satan wanted to exploit God's gift of the garden. He did it by an insinuating word in Eve's ear: 'Did God say...?' He subtly cast doubt on the good, wholesome truth of the living God. That deceit at the heart of mankind was the source of distortion and lies: the tongue became the vehicle for Satan's negative kingdom.

Imagine the scene. The service ends, we stroll out of church or stand chatting over coffee in the hall. Maybe five people comment on the service: 'The worship was beautiful today', 'I felt so close to God', 'Aren't we fortunate to have such a good singing group?' But it only needs one person to hint that things aren't that great and we'll go home feeling down because that one little thing outweighs all the positive things. Whenever we speak negatively, we abandon our weapons and open the gates for Satan's negative kingdom to rush in.

*The language of the revolution*

After the revolution in Libya, Colonel Gadaffi took over. Since then, his government has systematically rejected the English language and culture. School text books and library books in English have been thrown out; young people who have learned English in school and university are told to speak only Arabic languages – the language of the revolution. University students in their final years were allowed to finish their courses, but other courses have been scrapped because English is being phased out. In effect, the government says, 'We want the Arabic nations to keep together; we won't even have English taught in our schools. We will have the language of the revolution.'

When we come to know Jesus, we come into a new kingdom – the kingdom of God. We are in his revolution. We learn a new, positive language and lifestyle. Anyone who comes in with negative words and attitudes is allowing Satan a foothold – they aren't speaking the language of the revolution.

Of course, the trouble is that the church is far gentler than Colonel Gadaffi! In Libya the old language has been rejected – people are prevented from speaking it. Sometimes I think the church should prevent the language of Satan's kingdom from being heard. Clive Calver once wrote, 'With a church like this, who needs Satan?' Sad but true – we've dragged Satan's negative outlook into the church. We need to recall the words of the scripture, 'the one who is in you is greater than the one who is in the world' (1 Jn 4:4).

### The voice of criticism

I once attended a wonderful service; God's presence was powerful in the preaching and worship, and everyone was full of praise and joy. On the way out I heard someone say, 'God was with us in that service tonight – wasn't it fantastic?' And his friend replied, 'Yes, but I thought the offering was taken too slowly.' That comment was like bursting a balloon: we see all the blessings of God poured out, yet we still grumble about trivia.

People who talk like this often call themselves 'realists' – they think they have a gift for keeping other people's feet on the ground. It's their job to stop people getting too excited about their faith; to ring warning bells; to put up barriers; to say, 'On the other hand, you must remember this...and this.'

It's too easy for churches to become problem-orientated instead of God-orientated. God is always positive; he wants to move with power and authority in our world. But many churches are so crippled by a negative spirit that they are quite unable to face any challenge. In fact, Christians who have been filled with the power of the Holy Spirit are more at risk than anyone else, and for this reason: if Satan can't stop someone receiving the Holy Spirit's power, he'll take steps to divert it by making that person critical. I see this over and over again. People come to me in the first flush of the Spirit's power, saying 'I've been filled with the Spirit, praise the Lord.' But within two or three weeks they are back in my study, pointing the finger. They couch their objections in different language, of course, but basically what they're saying is, 'We've arrived, now get everybody else sorted out.'

We must face up to this fact of church life: any fool can criticise, and usually does! We state the problem as if it were the answer, and we can't tell the difference. Someone may go away from their house-group saying, 'Our group would be really great if we had a decent leader.' But that's not the answer – that's the problem. What is that person going to do about getting a decent leader? We know we should support and pray for our housegroup leader, but every time we say to other people, 'If only we had a good leader, we could really get it together,' we are sowing the seeds of destruction in that situation. We end up only with a caring group on the surface because it is full of Satan's negative spirit.

We may well want a decent housegroup leader; but then, our housegroup leader wants a decent group! We will get the person we want as we pray for them, support them and encourage them – in fact, as we bring God's positive kingdom into a negative situation. I remember a speaker at Spurgeon's College talking about this. He said, 'In any organisation you may find the leader does nine things you hate and one you love!' If you want to see God's positive kingdom established, you should go to the leader and focus on the one thing you appreciate, thank him for it and encourage him. When you build one another up in love, the positive is accentuated, and the nine bad things dwindle to eight, seven, six and so on.'

### Your reputation

What are you known for in your church – is it something positive or negative? When I visit and preach in different churches, I sometimes ask the deacons about the congregation. They reply, 'Well, there's Mr X – he doesn't like choruses; and Mrs Y – she's not very keen on...' People in the congregation are known for what they don't like or don't approve of.

Is your church being bred on a negative, critical spirituality? Do the people around you know you as the Porcupine because you bristle so much? Or do they think of you in a positive light? How much better if people can say of us, 'He's really committed to prayer...she's committed to worship...he's committed to evangelism.' It's a terrible indictment of our spiritual life if we are known only for our destructive and critical characteristics.

## A positive ministry

If ever there was a person who had a right to be critical, it was Jesus. The perfect and sinless one, only he could point the finger and criticise someone's life. But, remarkably, the gospels show that Jesus was almost entirely uncritical. He reserved his sharp remarks mainly for the Pharisees, but even for them he left the way open to reach him at a personal level.

Nicodemus was a Pharisee. Too embarrassed to approach Jesus openly, he went to him at night, secretly. Jesus didn't say to him, 'Go away, get back to the rest of your bunch of sinners – I don't want anything to do with you.' He gave him a warm welcome, answered his questions, and told him how he, too, could be put right with God. He offered words of hope and encouragement for Nicodemus' life, not destructive words.

What about the woman caught in the act of adultery? Can you imagine how that little incident would be received in the average church? Many of us would be on the phone: 'I'd just like to tell you this for your prayers....' Let's face it – some of us who call ourselves mature Christians can't resist passing on the juiciest bits of gossip, gloating over our brothers' and sisters' sins. But if our lives sink to that level, then we are back in Satan's negative kingdom, and all our worship counts for nothing.

How did Jesus deal with that woman? In his purity

and perfection he had every right to condemn her. What he actually said was, 'Let those without sin cast the first stone.' That got rid of the audience – they all slunk away guiltily, removing the threat of punishment and the opportunity for gossip. When Jesus was left alone with the woman he asked her where her accusers were. She looked around, saw they were gone, and heard those wonderful words: 'Neither do I condemn you – go and sin no more.' What he didn't say was, 'It's all right to live this way;' but, 'I'm not going to allow you to be stoned to death. The way you can best live is not to sin any more in that particular way.' Jesus offered her a positive word of guidance.

Jesus constantly exercised this positive ministry from God himself. Satan disfigures and destroys, but God brings his positive kingdom through his Son. Leprosy is a terrible, disfiguring disease: white marks appear on the skin. It is a numbing disease: the nerves are damaged so that fingers and toes lose their feeling, and this often results in severe injury because the warning signs of pain are lost. It is a crippling disease: hands often become claw-like and contracted so that the fingers can scarcely be prised open.

Jesus healed many lepers, and the act of healing them is a potent image of how he heals us of Satan's destructive work in our lives. He cleanses the marks of sin and disease; he restores feeling, love and joy; he straightens out our leprous fingers, opening our hands so that we can receive his gifts. Over and over again, Jesus healed the broken bodies and crushed spirits of those who came to him in first-century Palestine, just as he does today. The negative, destructive work of Satan's kingdom was replaced by wholeness. Throughout his ministry Jesus was constantly building, turning people from the negative to the positive.

*The nature of speech*

We need to be aware of the potential of our words, even our casual remarks, for good or ill. What would we lose if we all made a resolution not to talk to anyone in our church for a whole week? Many encouraging words would not be spoken, but neither would many harsh ones.

It's so much easier to say something negative than something positive. The worship in church last Sunday may have been lively, warm and enthusiastic – but it was a bit draughty, and the person next to you couldn't sing in tune, and you didn't really like those songs anyway (the minister never chooses your favourites) and aren't you supposed to keep your jacket on in church? A hundred negative things spring to mind immediately.

On a recent shopping trip to our local supermarket, I was struck by how much everyone was complaining. There I was with Bethany, my daughter, in one hand and a basket of things in the other, and as I went up and down the aisles I heard: 'They're always moving things round', 'Isn't it terrible weather?', 'This is more expensive than it was last week', 'I can never find a basket'. It was a really depressing trip! People love to whine and moan about even the most trivial things. And when we bring that attitude into church, we drag in some of the negative kingdom.

So our aim should be twofold: to be filled with the Spirit, and to get out of Satan's negative into God's positive. That way we can be sowers of life and light wherever we go, bringing encouraging words, not whingeing ones. We need to watch the tone in which we say things so that our comments are never aggressive, mean or harshly critical, but gentle, loving and positive.

*Constructive criticism*

This doesn't mean we have to pretend everything is perfect because we are afraid of offending anyone. It doesn't mean we are never allowed to criticise. If our tongues are ruled by God's positive teaching, that will sometimes mean correction or even rebuke but our criticism must be constructive, not carping or unthinking. It's relatively easy to distinguish between the two.

If we find something that needs correcting, we must put it right – but in God's way, with integrity, honesty and the courage of our convictions. A good guide is whom we tell: if we go away and talk about something to someone who can't do anything about it, then that's obviously not constructive criticism, it's just moaning. If we go and tell ten people who can't do anything about it, that's gossiping. But if we quietly approach someone in the right position and say, 'I wonder if this is right,' or, 'Could we possibly try this to build up our small groups, or our worship?' then we are being constructive – our positive attitude will help to build up the fellowship.

## God's positive kingdom

There are four main points to remember about our

tasks in God's positive kingdom. First, that the smallest negative remark can destroy the tone of a whole meeting. Even when things are going superbly, one unthinking, uncaring comment can spoil the atmosphere for everyone.

In our church we have many weddings. The bride always arrives looking beautiful in her special dress. But if there was just one black mark down the front of that dress, even a very thin one, the whole dress would be disfigured, and people would be embarrassed because everything wasn't quite right. The church is the bride of Christ, and we should take just as much care about the way we conduct ourselves in our fellowship as the bride does to be sure that her dress is perfect.

Secondly, we should only disapprove of sin. We shouldn't waste our disapproval on things which are merely a matter of taste. Some people sincerely believe that we will be singing *Songs of Fellowship* in heaven! Quite mistaken, of course, because the folk down the road know we'll be singing from *The Baptist Hymn Book* and it'll all be in Welsh! We need the gift of tolerance for other people's habits or fancies or cultures, and the wisdom to see our own tastes in the same light.

Thirdly, we have to break down the emotional barriers so that God can work. Criticism creates tension and pressure, whereas positive affirmation defuses emotional upheavals and frees us to worship the living God.

Finally, every Christian has a choice between three things, as far as God's positive kingdom is concerned. Recent television coverage of an earthquake showed ravaged buildings, which had taken so long to design and build, being demolished by bulldozers clearing the sites. All around people had gathered to watch the demolition, but right in the foreground, where the bulldozers hadn't reached, there were men digging frantically with their bare hands, looking for anyone still alive under the rubble.

In that scene I saw a picture of the kingdom of God: there were the destroyers, the positive discoverers of life, and the observers. We can be the destroyers, using our tongues to ruin years of work in a moment. Or we can be observers, which is only slightly better, just standing back to watch what happens. Or we can be the positive builders, bringing hope and health and vitality to God's people.

If we make the right choices, guarding our tongues and looking for opportunities to build, we can help to bring in the joy and the glory of God's positive kingdom.

# 2

## Suffering

One of the most evident signs of Satan's negative kingdom in our world is suffering. Whether from illness, accident, distress or fear – we suffer and our loved ones suffer. Throughout history theologians and philosophers have struggled with this fact, yet for two thousand years Christians have found victory in the worst kinds of anguish because Jesus has been real to them.

At the academic level the problem of suffering is complex, even insoluble, yet beyond the academic there is a solution in the heart of God: it is not revealed in its entirety to man because our minds are finite, while God is infinite. Yet there are moments when we are close to God when we almost comprehend the love which lies beyond the suffering of this world.

Recently I visited an old lady in the old people's home where she lives. When I last saw her, she weighed twelve stones; now, a few months later, she weighed six stones. We talked for a while and then she reached out a hand to me and said, 'Stephen, pray that I may die.' She is frail and incontinent, almost senile; she is a believer, but depressed and discouraged. She wants to go to be with God. In that heart cry, I recognised the intense suffering which so many people face. We cannot refuse to think about this suffering, or make a half-hearted attempt at it – or worse, approach it with superficial trium-phalism. 'Just praise God and it will go away' is utterly out of step with the teaching of the Scrip-tures; a 'Smile, God loves you' sticker on your car rear window will not help anyone in pain.

We need to think about this seriously if we are to be open for God to bring us relief in our suffering, now or in the future.

## What causes suffering?

### A fallen world

The book of Genesis is fundamental to our under-standing of suffering, because there we see God's created beings – Adam and Eve – in a world which is flawless. Sin comes into the world through their rebellion and the world falls. The results of a fallen creation are clear: 'It will produce thorns and this-tles for you, and you will eat the plants of the field' (Gen 3:18).

Thorns and thistles may not seem very relevant to us in the twentieth century, but look more closely. Man's original sin brought about decay in the per-fect created order. The writer of the book of Genesis uses weeds and thistles to illustrate that essential change in creation. He says, in effect, creation used to be marvellous, roses just came up everywhere and one never had to weed the garden. But then sin came into the world and nature went from being the pure, gentle gift of God – the lion lying down with the lamb, to the violent and bloody nature we know, with its volcanoes, earthquakes, tidal waves and other natural disasters.

The creation needs to be redeemed, just as humanity needs to be redeemed. That is why the letter to the Romans tells us that the whole creation groans, waiting for the day when a new heaven and a new earth will come. Then all the cosmic disorders will be undone by Jesus, and the world will be renewed and recreated in its original perfection. But meanwhile, the distortion of the natural order brings about a whole range of problems which cause us suffering.

## A fallen humanity

Mankind is closely linked with the fallen creation. Paul wrote: 'Therefore, just as sin entered the world through one man, and death through sin, and in this way death came to all men, because all sinned' (Rom 5:12). In the beginning God created a man in his own image; that man chose, with his wife, to rebel against God. At that moment Adam became the channel through which sin flowed into creation and into his offspring. We are part of fallen humanity. When you point one finger at the rest of the world, three fingers of your own hand point back at you (try it!). We are all involved in the guilt of humanity.

Of course, we aren't directly responsible for the suffering in, say, Northern Ireland. But we do share the sinful nature common to all humanity – selfishness, pride, a nature which is twisted and bent out of contact with God – that is responsible for such pain.

The Christian message declares that a twisted humanity can be taken by Jesus and stretched on the rack of his love: sometimes it's painful, but we can be pulled to the point of uprightness by the power of the Spirit. The image of God in us can be restored in Jesus. Yet before we can accept this truth for ourselves we have to understand that suffering comes through a fallen humanity of which we are all a part.

While we are looking at this issue, it's worth remarking that there are only two kinds of people: those who are part of the problem, and those who are part of the solution. Those who are part of the problem have never had God's life come in and stretch them out and transform them into the image of Christ. But when we become Christians we place ourselves in the hands of the original maker, and he remakes us in his image.

Some time ago I watched a demonstration at the Wedgewood factory in Stoke-on-Trent. It was fascinating to watch the clay on the wheel being moulded by skilful hands, changing into a pot in front of our eyes. Sometimes it flopped to one side, or didn't turn out quite right, so the potter just pushed it all back down on to the wheel, wetted it, and began again.

Jeremiah talks about the potter and the clay to illustrate the point that when we offer ourselves back to

God he begins to remake us. He alone can take our bent, spoiled shapes and mould us again into his image. The suffering in the world that comes from our rebellion against God can only be relieved if we move into a right relationship with God and allow him to reshape our lives.

## The work of Satan

'You belong to your father, the devil, and you want to carry out your father's desire. He was a murderer from the beginning, not holding to the truth, for there is no truth in him. When he lies, he speaks his native language, for he is a liar and the father of lies' (Jn 8:44).

Sometimes people say to me, 'How can you believe in a God of love, with all the suffering in the world?' My answer is, 'How can you bear to live your life in a world this awful without believing in God?' Let me expand on this point. When I look at the Scriptures, I see a source for much of this suffering – Satan, God's adversary.

The Bible is full of images of warfare between evil and good, and the evil focuses on Satan. Anyone who doesn't believe in God must simply see a malevolent world force. Suffering then appears spontaneous, irrational and random. To reject the Christian worldview is to condemn yourself to one which is utterly meaningless; your only hope is that misfortunes will somehow miss you and you'll be lucky enough to live to a reasonably happy old age and die and return to the dust.

Whatever the problems faced by Christians, they are nothing compared to those faced by non-Christians who attempt to explain what happens in the world. The Christian can say with confidence that Satan is the author of much that is evil.

The book of Job describes how Satan is wandering around on the face of the earth, and then attacks God's servant Job. Look anywhere in the Scriptures and you will see the work of the enemy, the father of lies and the king of evil.

That is why, as Christians, we must recognise that very often the battle against suffering is the battle against evil, against Satan and all his forces. It is very important to grasp that Satan is a personality, because to ignore your enemy is to put yourself at a disadvantage. Imagine how Churchill would have behaved in the Second World War if he had looked at the reports of the invasion of Poland and said, 'There is something evil going on in Europe, but I don't believe in Hitler.' In fact, Churchill's memoirs show that he tried to find out about Hitler's character and personality and learn how his mind worked so that he could predict and counter-attack. We, too, should remember that we are fighting a real adversary in the devil.

A word of caution here: Satan enjoys free publicity, so let's not give him any. He enjoys being the focus of attention, so let's not give him that pleasure. We should focus on Jesus. We should recognise our enemy, but not become so obsessed by him that we see a demon round every corner. It's a sad fact that many people who are in conflict with Satan in the ministry of exorcism may become very harsh and intolerant; there are many reasons for this, but one is the inability to step back from a situation and see Jesus as King.

We need caution in dealing with Satan, but we need to recognise that he is the enemy.

## Does God send suffering?

To be frank, I'm not sure about the answer to this question; the best way to answer it is to look at the Bible. The Old Testament shows a God who visits the enemies of his people with plagues, famine and death. In God's dealing with his people he seems to be allowing suffering, rather than sending it.

This is taught most clearly in the book of Job. Satan goes to God and says, 'Of course Job worships you – I would, too, if I had 250 camels, four servants, six wives, two dogs and a parrot. What else do you expect?' And God says, 'Well, all right, you can take all that away from him, but you can't touch his body.' God allows Job to be tested. Then, in Chapter 2, Satan returns. God says, 'Have you seen Job? You took all those things away from him and he still trusts me.' And Satan says, 'Yes, but look at him, he has health and strength and energy. Once he starts suffering he'll complain – you know what men are like once they get a little headache.' So Job is attacked physically, and still he doesn't crack.

God allowed suffering to come upon one of his people, and I believe that the truth of the biblical pattern is this: God does not send suffering but he sometimes allows it so that the church as a body may identify with the sufferings of Jesus, and so that we as individual Christians may mature in the faith.

This view of suffering can be very helpful to us. It means that all Christians have an 'umbrella' over them which may be called God's will or God's love.

We can be sure that nothing is allowed through that protection except by God's permission.

## Why does God allow suffering?

If pain is sometimes permitted by God, what are the reasons for it? What is God doing when this happens? The answer falls into four parts.

*Free will*

This is a very old argument from Scripture. If God had made us all like robots, he could have programmed us to do his will; because he chose instead to give us freedom to love him, he can't guarantee what we will do.

Someone once asked me, 'Is there anything that God can't do?' They were pretty surprised when I answered yes. He can't make two and two equal five, because he created the world to have a certain order. He can't act selfishly, and he can't sin – not because it's beyond his power, but because it's outside his nature. And he can't create humanity with free will and also insist on it behaving perfectly, because the two things aren't compatible.

When God gave us free will, he also gave us the responsibility that goes with it. He gave us real freedom, so that every time we have freedom to choose, the possibility is opened up for rejecting God and bringing about sin and suffering. God gave us freedom because he wants our love, not our slavish service. The letter to the Galatians says, 'You are no longer a slave, but a son' (Gal 4:7), and that's what worship is all about – freely giving ourselves and our love to God, not being dominated by him.

Because we are free there is bound to be suffering, because we are sinful people.

*A sense of mystery*

Why is it that some people suffer and others do not? Why are some people plagued by problems while others seem to be problem-free? As a pastor, I'm always being asked that question. My honest answer is that I don't know.

There are a great many things we don't know about God; we need to remember that he is a mystery. Our response to the things that only God knows is trust and faith. We may not understand why things are happening to us, but if we love God and believe in him, we know that he will act rightly.

In *The Hiding Place*, Corrie Ten Boom tells a story about a question she asked her father. He felt that she wasn't old enough to understand the response to the question, so he put down the suitcase he was carrying and said to her, 'Pick up that case.' She knew she wasn't strong enough to lift it, and he said, 'Quite,' and picked it up and carried it for her. He pointed out that just as the case was too heavy for her to carry right now, some things were too hard for her to understand; but one day, everything would be revealed. The issue of suffering is that kind of problem – when we meet God in heaven we will understand it.

Two friends of mine were devastated when their baby was born severely handicapped by Down's Syndrome. They wept and prayed together, wondering how they were going to cope with this child and all his needs. The father told me, 'I looked into God's face and cried, "Why?" And there was no answer from heaven, but I saw a picture of Jesus in my mind, and he was crying too. In that moment I had a glimpse of the whole mystery of suffering: although I couldn't have an answer to my question, I knew that God loved me and cared intensely for me in my suffering, and that was marvellous.'

The 'why' of suffering is found in the love of God, and sometimes we can find an answer nowhere else.

### Perfecting the saints

Those who have never suffered will never really grow spiritually. The old saints used to call it 'the dark night of the soul'. Until our natures have been sculpted by the hammer of affliction and the chisel of pressure and temptation and grief and pain, our spirits will be surrounded by such a thick layer of ego that God can't penetrate it. But as we suffer and put ourselves in God's hands, the selfish parts of our personalities are chipped away until the spirit is released, and we are revealed as men and women of God, made in his image.

I think I can safely say that in all the history of the church there has never been a great saint of God, man or woman, who hasn't experienced suffering in one form or another. It's through the fire of affliction that the spiritual person is revealed.

### An evangelistic tool

Sometimes God uses suffering as a warning bell to a busy world, to rouse people into asking the questions about life and death that can bring them to his great answer. Suffering brings some people into the church to hear the good news of Jesus Christ, and from there into the kingdom of God.

## What can we do about it?

Even when we have considered what causes suffering and why God allows it, another question arises: what can we do about it? What steps can we take as Christians to respond to the problem?

### Discover its source

The first step is to ask yourself why you are suffering. For example, is it because you're stupid? That is actually a serious question. Maybe you've been going to bed at 3 am for a week or going out without a mac and getting soaked. If you have, and you're ill, then you can't expect much sympathy. We need to be quite clear that there are some things which we bring upon ourselves.

### See God's response

This next step is the crucial one, especially with regard to healing. It's not a sin to be sick, but it's a sin to be sicker than we ought to be. If we truly seek God's response, we will find that he wants to heal and bring victory more often than we do, not less. When we hear what God is saying, we can move with confidence and authority and pray in faith. But we have to think things through, not just pray trite and superficial prayers.

There are two opposite attitudes concerning this issue, and I believe both are unbiblical. The first extreme says, 'If only we have enough faith, everyone will be healed and all the suffering will disappear.' The second says, 'We're all human, and suffering is part of life so we just have to put up with it.'

Neither of those views is true to the New Testament. The joy of the Christian life lies in discovering God's response, in praying and seeing God's healing and victory worked out in our situation. If we seek God's power and watch him at work, we shall see the kingdom of darkness and suffering pushed back by the kingdom of light.

### This world is not the end

For the Christian, all suffering has meaning because this life is not the end – it's just the beginning. Whether we have sixty, seventy, eighty years or more, it is all preparation for eternity. When we realise this, we view suffering in a different perspective – in the light of all the great things God is going to do in the future. As Paul declares, 'I consider that our present sufferings are not worth comparing with the glory that will be revealed in us'(Rom 8:18). In the strength of Christ, we can face any troubles secure in the promises of God.

# 3

## *Emotional Wholeness*

Now there is in Jerusalem near the Sheep gate a pool,
which in Aramaic is called Bethesda and which is surrounded by five covered colonnades. Here a great
number of disabled people used to lie – the blind, the
lame, the paralysed. One who was there has been an
invalid for thirty-eight years. When Jesus saw him lying
there and learned that he had been in this condition for
a long time, he asked him, 'Do you want to get well?'

'Sir,' the invalid replied, 'I have no one to help me
into the pool when the water is stirred. While I am trying to get in, someone else goes down ahead of me.'

Then Jesus said to him, 'Get up! Pick up your mat
and walk.' At once the man was cured; he picked up his
mat and walked (Jn 5:2–9).

At first sight this appears to be another story about
suffering, and God's power to intervene in our lives
and heal the physically disabled. But there is more to
it. In this passage the reading of the Authorised

Version is preferable to that of the NIV because the word 'wholeness' is used here: Jesus' question to the man is not a superficial 'Do you want to get well?' but 'Do you want to be made whole [or complete]?'

A second Bible passage is relevant to our thinking on this subject:

> It was he who gave some to be apostles, some to be prophets, some to be evangelists, and some to be pastors and teachers, to prepare God's people for works of service, so that the body of Christ may be built up until we all reach unity in the faith and in the knowledge of the Son of God and become mature, attaining to the whole measure of the fullness of Christ.
>
> Then we will no longer be infants, tossed back and forth by the waves, and blown here and there by every wind of teaching and by the cunning and craftiness of men in their deceitful scheming. Instead, speaking the truth in love, we will in all things grow up into him who is the head, that is, Christ (Eph 4:11–15).

Paul places maturity high on the agenda, and so should we. Most church leaders admit that a large proportion of their pastoral problems arise from the emotional immaturity of the fellowship they serve. There is a tragic childishness about our emotional and spiritual lives which often wrecks the high ideals we aim for. We all need to study the word of God and use it as the basis for our thinking about emotional maturity.

## Damaged emotions

Practically everyone has been hurt in some way.

Many people long to wave a magic wand over their emotional life and have it settled and calm. Many more of us, though basically 'together' as people, find that in certain situations we react emotionally instead of spiritually – we may be angry with ourselves afterwards, yet we never seem to conquer that particular failing. Almost everyone you meet suffers from damaged or uncontrolled emotions.

Theologically, of course, it's true of all of us. When Adam and Eve fell from grace in the garden, not only were their will and their reasoning capacity damaged, but also their emotions: we have inherited faulty emotions from our forebears.

At the same time, certain events in our lives make the condition worse, and that may happen in two ways: crisis damage and process damage.

*Crisis damage*

This kind of damage is caused by the sudden, unexpected event. It is rather like the physical damage caused by an accident in which you break your leg. There is a sudden trauma, a great deal of shock and pain, and then, slowly, healing begins. You may not be aware of the healing at first, but with time and proper care you should recover.

Crisis emotional damage is similar: your life may be perfectly all right, then something happens which crushes your spirit until you feel damaged beyond repair. This afternoon I was working in my study when there was a howl of wind outside. In one moment my back gate was ripped off its hinges and thrown to the ground. A crisis may be a bereavement. Someone you loved dearly is suddenly taken from you, and you experience loss and pain such as you never imagined, like a knife permanently inside you, wounding you.

Maybe it's discovering that your husband or wife has been unfaithful – something that happens even to Christians. Or perhaps you've been made redundant, with little hope of another job. Whatever it may be, disaster strikes and you feel damaged: you can't worship properly, you can't relate to people properly, every aspect of your life is affected.

When something like this happens, you can only turn to Christ, who was brutally hammered to a cross on Calvary. He reaches out to us with his love and says, 'I know how you feel. I know rejection, loss, loneliness – yes, even death. I've been through life's crises and I understand your emotional pain.' But the trouble is this: you may have thought you had a fruitful relationship with God, but often when you are at that point of crisis, you turn to him and he's not there. Or, more accurately, you can't feel him.

C.S.Lewis wrote in *A Grief Observed* about his feelings after the death of his wife, Joy. In the film *Shadowlands* he was shown talking to the minister who conducted her funeral: the clergyman said, 'Well, Jack, just have faith.'

And Lewis replied, 'Look, I've called out to God and all I've heard was the sound of a heavenly door being closed, bolted and double-bolted on the inside, and then silence.'

He had prayed to the God he loved and trusted, but in the pain of that moment God seemed farther away than ever before.

This seems to be a universal experience: at the moment of our deepest need, we find it hardest to reach God. It's like the crashing sound of a huge orchestra playing – the noises of pain, loss, hopelessness and conflicting advice confuse us, and we fail to hear the word of God, which is like a treble recorder situated somewhere behind the drums. The jangling of our own emotions in our hearts and minds makes us deaf to the gentle tune of the Spirit playing in our lives.

But just because we can't hear the piper, that doesn't mean he isn't playing. If we can only wait for the emotions to subside a little, we will be able to hear God's voice again. It's like the old story of the dream. A man walks along a beach which seems to be the path of his life, and the Lord Jesus is beside him. He looks back the way they have come and says, 'Jesus, at the worst times in my life I can see only one set of footprints. You promised to be with me always – so why did you leave me then?' And Jesus replies, 'My son, in those times, I was carrying you.'

We may feel alone at a time of crisis, and that can make our sufferings worse; but we can trust our Lord not to leave us. He loves us and longs to bring his healing to us, so that we can hear his voice again.

*Process damage*

Fortunately, the crises of life don't happen all the time. But we may suffer another kind of emotional damage – process damage. If crisis damage is sudden, process damage tends to develop over a long period, like cancer. The illness starts somewhere, of course, but its effects emerge gradually. While crisis damage tends to heal in time, process damage tends to get worse, partly because we get used to it. We may not realise we need help, or the damage seems so much part of us that we don't believe we can be helped. We say it's just our bad temper or our abrasive and hurtful manner. Whatever the excuses we make for these little failings of ours – 'I just tell the truth, I can't help it if people get upset'; 'I can't help flying off the handle when I'm tired' – the fact remains that God wants to deal with our inner turmoil and bring us through to emotional maturity.

This brings us to the second misconception about the state of our emotions – that they are somehow separate from our spiritual life, which is all God is interested in. It's too easy to think that all you have to do is 'get saved', that God is only concerned with the spirit. That is why the passage from John 5 is so important, because Jesus asks, 'Do you want to be made whole?' (v 6). The word there is 'complete' – not just, 'Do you want your legs to work again?' So when the NIV says, 'At once the man was cured' the actual words are, 'At once the man was made whole' – complete.

Jesus is not just interested in saving your soul, as if it existed separately from the rest of you. He wants to redeem the whole of you – your mind, your will, your personality, everything that makes you the individual you are, because that is whom Jesus loves – the person that is you. He wants to bring your emotions to maturity so that you can attain 'to the whole measure of the fullness of Christ'.

## Dealing with emotions

None of us is perfect; everyone has to cope with immature or damaged emotions which affect us every day in all we do. How do we deal with these powerful feelings which can damage our spiritual lives?

### Choking the dog

Emotions are like a dog on a lead: if the lead is too tight, the dog will choke. Many of us keep our emotions reined in so tightly that we are actually choking them.

Although it's a generalisation, this matter of reining in the emotions is especially a problem for men. It's partly due to our society – we are taught that men are meant to be strong, and that to show emotion is weak. The result is that many men are too restrained, refusing to acknowledge that they have any emotional life at all. Perhaps they are nervous of freedom in worship, in case it becomes 'too emotional'; perhaps they don't like to be around when anyone gets upset; perhaps they avoid people who have been bereaved; perhaps they never cry. They are choking the dog.

Let's nail once and for all the myth that men don't cry. God isn't calling us to hysterical outbursts, but he is calling us to emotional freedom, which will bring the warmth of our hearts into our worship. That may or may not bring us to tears, but it will release us from fear and embarrassment and bring us into emotional wholeness.

*The runaway heart*

The opposite error, of course, is to keep the dog on too loose a lead so that it runs away unrestrained, chasing around and dragging us behind it. When our emotions are out of control we have no stability: one day our attitudes are governed by one thing, the next by another. This problem is considered to be more common among women.

One idea which has some currency among both men and women is what we might call the 'Let it all hang out' theory of emotions. An interesting study was performed in Philadelphia, monitored by sociologists and psychologists. They brought together groups of people who disagreed with others, through anger, prejudice, etc, and encouraged them to confront one another with their feelings, releasing their anger and shouting. What they discovered was that the people who had expressed their anger freely didn't feel any better afterwards: by rehearsing their feelings over and over again they had actually reinforced them rather than dispersed them.

*In God's hands*

There is a third way of dealing with our emotions, and that is to hand them over to God. We have to find the balance between controlling our emotions and being controlled by them, and that balance is perfectly held in God's hands. We need to put God in charge of our emotional life.

I am constantly amazed at the number of Christians I meet who have given God control of their work life and devotional life, but whose emotional life is a mess. Everything may appear to be in order, but deep down there is turmoil because of this area which is not under the sovereign control of Jesus Christ. The solution to the problem of spiritual immaturity is not found in gritting your teeth and holding back all emotion, nor in letting your feelings run away with you, but in letting God control your emotions by his power and presence.

The fact is that our emotions make good servants but poor masters. If they are in charge, we change our direction as the wind blows; if God is in charge, our emotions bring warmth, colour and variety into our lives.

When I was in America I decided to get married, but there were many processes involved in that one decision. I wanted to do God's will, so I prayed for guidance – that was the spiritual dimension. I thought about it a great deal. Would our lives be compatible? What would this woman be like as the home-maker and the mother of our children – that was the rational dimension. Then my will came into play. I decided I would ask her to marry me; I was going to will it all to happen, in line with God's will.

But it would be a sorry affair if that were all there was; there had to be some emotional content. I can still remember how nervous I was about asking her, the sign of the deeper emotion of love which made the will and the reason come alive. The point is that the emotions were a part of all this decision-making. I wouldn't have married her if I hadn't loved her as well!

Yet emotions can vary, and there are days in any

marriage when the warm feelings are not so strong. They are a totally unreliable guide to the state of your marriage. If the emotions were taken as the ruling factor, you'd get a divorce every time you had indigestion.

You can't run your life by your emotions alone. You run it by your will and your reason and your emotions together, under the sovereign guidance of God's Holy Spirit. God has to be in control.

## Emotional immaturity

Look for a moment at what happens when God is not allowed to deal with the emotional side of our lives. People whose emotions are out of control hurt themselves, because they have no peace. They hurt other people, who never know quite how to relate to them ('What kind of mood is he in today?'). And they hurt the church because non-Christians look at them and say, 'If that's what Christianity is like I don't want it.' That can add up to quite a lot of damage from just one 'unimportant' area of your life. Your emotional immaturity can turn you into a walking disaster area!

Of course, that can't mean you – can it? If you think you aren't included in this description, think again – you may possibly be one of the worst offenders. It's too easy to ignore our own problems and point a finger at others; it's the people who recognise and confess their own weaknesses who are moving slowly in the right direction. So check yourself for symptoms of immaturity right away!

*Checking for symptoms*

The first symptom is moodiness. If you don't always relate to people in the same way, check whether something is dominating your relationships other than Jesus. You don't have to be a great extrovert or the life and soul of the party all the time – you may be very quiet and shy. But if you don't respond to people open-heartedly and consistently, then you have a problem.

You know the scene: something upsets you. You go to church just the same because it's the right thing to do, but you sit there and look as black as thunder, refusing to participate fully. You've been hurt and you intend to get full value out of it. It affects the people around you and it affects the spirit of the service as a whole.

We all have days when our moods change, but inflicting them on other people is immature. It's a sign that God is not influencing that part of our behaviour.

The second symptom often masks itself as spirituality, so it may be harder to spot: a tendency to muddle emotional feelings with spiritual truth. Some Christians cover their emotional insecurity by saying things like, 'The Lord said,' 'I feel led,' 'I have a real peace about,' or 'I feel a sense of'. It sounds very convincing but it's very dangerous because most of us like to take our feelings and pin on a label saying 'from God'.

When I was younger, I remember attending a church seminar on 'bringing everything to God', and not doing anything unless one 'felt led'. Looking back, I suppose they were referring to major decisions like getting married or choosing a career. When I arrived home my mother was making supper 'Steve,' she asked, 'will you lay the table?'

'Well,' I replied, 'I don't have a real peace about that.'

'I don't care whether you've got peace or not,' she said. 'Lay the table!'

Pseudo-spiritual people can be very tiresome. If you are asked to put out some chairs, you don't have to go away and pray for three weeks to see if you feel led. It doesn't matter if you don't feel like giving out the hymnbooks, just do it!

This vague feeling of being led to do things can be a disastrous approach to Christian living: it elevates our emotions to the place of the Spirit. It conveniently bypasses more down-to-earth and biblical issues like duty, obedience and fairness. God doesn't always speak to our emotions; sometimes he speaks to our minds, through the Bible or through a friend. We may indeed 'feel led' to things quite legitimately, but we must take care that we don't manipulate God's word to us.

### Healing the heart

Once we have learned to release our emotions, or restrain our emotions, and bring them under God's control, what then? How can we attain emotional maturity? I believe that just as there are two kinds of emotional damage – crisis and process damage, so there are two steps in the healing process – a crisis point and a longer process.

First, God wants to touch each one of us and heal our hurts. If we ask him, he is ready at any moment to come into our lives, to warm and enliven our hearts, or to calm and soothe them, and to begin to govern our emotions. Just as the sudden crisis causes damage, crisis-point healing can happen in a moment.

But that is not the end. Many emotional habits develop over a lifetime – one experience won't break them. That is not doubting the power of God, it's knowing human nature. Anything that depends on the exercise of a little will-power takes time to get established! With process damage, long-term healing is needed. You need to go on inviting the living God into your life, day by day.

You may need other help, as well, and you shouldn't be afraid to take it, whether it's counselling or medication. At a time of crisis you may need both Valium and prayer, and fear should not prevent you from taking advice from either your GP or your minister. But the process healing must follow on – letting God guide you step by step to wholeness.

So whatever the damage in our lives, whether we are prone to depression, bad temper, lying or moodiness, we need to turn to God, for his healing touch now, and his daily help and inspiration as we continue to give our emotions back to him. He wants us to be whole, to be complete, to be mature in Christ – something that can happen only as our emotions come under the hand of God.

# 4

## *The Principle of Discontinuity*

In the last chapter we looked at emotional wholeness. This issue raises one of the misconceptions
about our human condition: the inability to change.
We may not say it aloud, because that sounds as if we
are doubting God's power, but deep down we
believe that there is something in us – some problem
or anxiety, some personality trait – that even God
can't change. It's an idea current in society, too: that
behaviour is determined by our genes or our envi-
ronment, factors outside our control, and that therefore certain patterns are part of the nature of
humanity. Starvation and suffering will never be
eradicated because of greed and selfishness: that's
what the human race is like.

Sometimes this thinking infiltrates the church,
too, so that we just give up in certain areas: we think
we can't affect things because we or other people
can't alter those flaws in our characters. We'll always
have to work around certain people because they

will always be bad tempered – it's just the way they are.

But this kind of thinking is quite wrong, for the reason I gave before: the God who created order out of chaos is all-powerful; he can bring our chaotic, fallen lives into the glory of his order.

## The unchanging God

God never fails. The Bible assures us that the God of the Old Testament is the God of the New Testament. The God who created the world and who created the church is the God of the twentieth century, and is the same God through the ages until the day when he forms a new heaven and a new earth. Jesus Christ is the same yesterday, today and for ever (Heb 13:8) – there is no shadow of changing with God.

My grandfather was a local preacher, and although we differed about many things, we shared this belief. We expressed the gospel in quite different ways, but we believed in the same Jesus. Whatever our age, Jesus is the same for all of us, and he is the same on the day we die as on the day we were born. The way we express our faith may change, the way we evangelise or worship may change, but Jesus Christ remains the same. In that knowledge we may rest secure.

It is precisely because God is unchanging and continuous that the principle of *discontinuity* is possible for men and women in every age. Put simply, the principle is this: God can change us. Things need not always remain as they are now, and this is true both of the individual personality and of the corporate church.

## Altering the individual

> Listen, I tell you a mystery: we will not all sleep, but we will all be changed – in a flash, in the twinkling of an eye, at the last trumpet. For the trumpet will sound, the dead will be raised imperishable, and we will be changed. For the perishable must clothe itself with the imperishable, and the mortal with immortality. When the perishable has been clothed with the imperishable, and the mortal with immortality, then the saying that is written will come true: 'Death has been swallowed up in victory.' 'Where, O death, is your victory? Where, O death, is your sting?' The sting of death is sin, and the power of sin is the law. But thanks be to God! He gives us the victory through our Lord Jesus Christ (1 Cor 15:51–57).

> But whenever anyone turns to the Lord, the veil is taken away. Now the Lord is the Spirit, and where the Spirit of the Lord is, there is freedom. And we, who with unveiled faces all reflect the Lord's glory, are being transformed into his likeness with ever-increasing glory, which comes from the Lord, who is the Spirit (2 Cor 3:16–18).

The first passage is describing the change at the end of time: we aren't going to be perfect this side of heaven. Paul writes to the Corinthians and says, 'We will not all sleep but we will all be changed,' and then there is a pause and he adds 'in a flash' rather as though he were amazed at the thought.

Like any student of human nature, Paul knows that in the ordinary course of events, people don't change overnight. When God comes into our life he can fill us with his Holy Spirit in a moment, but the outworking of that takes a lifetime. So the wonder of this passage is the idea that one day we will be transformed, suddenly, by God. That's a marvellous thing to look forward to: a time when every struggle with sin or sickness will be over, and we will be made like Christ.

In the second passage, however, Paul talks about the standard way God operates. We are being transformed 'into his likeness with ever-increasing glory'. In the RSV this verse reads, 'Changed from one degree of glory into another.' It takes a lifetime for God to change us.

This principle of the possibility of change is central to Scripture – the only problem is that I find it hard to believe for myself. I can believe it all right for other people: I can preach about it and counsel and comfort others with this great hope – whatever your problem, God can deal with it. It's always easier to believe in this principle for other people than for yourself: after all, only you know just what you are really like. It's at this point that we have to go back to the Bible. It's full of stories of real people with real problems and real sins – and if God's power for change could be true for them, it can be true for us.

*David*

David, the mighty warrior king of the Old Testament, became guilty of two grave sins – murder and adultery – in a very short period of time. These sins could have overshadowed David's life and made him useless to God, but for the prophet Nathan. Nathan understood the principle of discontinuity and challenged David to repent. In those days, to tell a king that he was a sinner was a very risky business, but Nathan dared because he believed in the possibility of change.

We know what happens after sin: despair follows distress, we feel useless and spoiled. We can imagine the kind of thing the devil was saying to David then: 'You've sinned now, you'll never get back in favour with God. He can't forgive this – murder and adultery in a man supposed to be God's anointed king? You're finished now. You'll never be asked to do anything significant for God ever again.' Satan, of course, is a great believer in the continuity of the effects of sin – it suits him very well.

Perhaps you have experienced an adulterous relationship, or some less obvious breach of trust, or you have stolen something from your place of work. Whatever it is, if you believe in Satan's continuity you will never get rid of the guilt feelings. It may have happened ten or twenty years ago, but you feel your life has never been the same since. As long as you don't let your mind wander to that sin, you can worship freely and joyfully. But as soon as your mind is free, it dwells on that sin. You feel hurt and bruised; the victorious Christian life you'd like to live evades you.

This is where the principle of discontinuity comes in. When David accepted responsibility for his sin, he should have been written off – but he wasn't. Nathan spoke up and called him to repentance, and through that repentance God raised David up and by his power he changed the kind of king he was. Whatever the sin, God can come in to redirect your life and transform it into the glorious life he wants it to be. It's like the great blob of paint dropped by accident onto a canvas, which is transformed by the artist into part of the picture: by his skill the painter incorporates the mistake into the glorious whole.

When God has finished with our lives we won't be able to see the dirt or the sin or the mistakes – only the likeness of Christ which he has drawn there. And that power for change and transformation is available because of the continuity of the living God.

## Job

When we consider Job we see not a sinner but a sufferer. Many of us can probably identify with him. Maybe we have lost a partner, or been hurt and betrayed, or endured some physical or mental illness. Time passes and the critical agony lessens, but underneath we are still hurting. We feel we will never recover, we will never be useful to God again, because all our energy is taken up with just keeping going.

It may seem obvious that you will be crippled for the rest of your life by this suffering – it may be that there is still more suffering to come – but God can prevent you from being in bondage to it. He can transform your life so that you don't wake each morning dreading what the day will bring, because 'the Lord blessed the latter part of Job's life more than the first'.

## Peter

Peter denied his Lord three times; that must make him one of the greatest failures. One of our biggest personal problems, it seems to me, is that we feel that we are failures. We try over and over again to get things right, but we never do. We struggle with the wrong things we say, the wrong things we do, the wrong things we think. We don't read our Bibles or pray as we ought, we feel our worship is second-rate and haphazard, and we miss out on what God has for us. Most of all, we don't really expect things ever to change. We think we 'll always get it wrong, that some areas of our lives are just doomed to be second-best.

The third time Jesus appeared to the disciples after his death, he had a meal with them. And then he had a little chat with Peter, who was probably feeling pretty low.

'I'm sorry, Lord, I really failed you. I can't look you in the eye. I feel really bad.'

'Peter, on your leadership and your testimony I'm going to build my whole church, and you're going to be the leading apostle.'

Peter must have looked over his shoulder to see if Jesus was talking to someone else. Peter, a failure, denying Jesus, was to lead the church.

In the same way, God is ready to come into every one of our failures and use us in ways we couldn't dream possible. Jesus is concerned when we fail, but he doesn't wait for us to stop failing before he uses us, he just waits for us to come back to him. Things don't have to go on as they are. The principle of discontinuity means that we can break away from the old paths, because there is no problem too great for God to deal with.

## Changing the church

However, even when we accept that we can be changed on a personal level, it's sometimes hard to believe that the church can be changed on a corporate level. There seems to be so much more inertia in a large number of people!

When I first came to my present church, I had a vision of what could happen there in terms of worship, growth, social care and action. I thought the worship would be marvellous, the church would be full of glowing evangelists, and all I'd have to do would be to pop up and preach for a few minutes now and then. The whole town would be affected by our witness and the community changed to God's honour and glory.

I wonder if you would be surprised to hear that most of this hasn't happened yet?

I don't know the reasons why: perhaps the vision wasn't right, perhaps I failed to communicate it, perhaps the congregation was a little stubborn. Whatever the cause, the important thing is that I have to go on believing in the principle of discontinuity: that just because radical change hasn't happened so far, that doesn't mean that it can't or won't happen, this week or next week or some other time.

There are churches everywhere where people are frustrated because things don't seem to be changing; yet within the same churches there are people who are distressed because things seem to them to be changing too much. They may see spiritual gifts being exercised, or hear music groups singing new songs; they see dancers or mime artists moving around, contributing to the service, and they are alarmed. It may be that they don't like the pace of change in the outside world either, and have turned to the church for security and changelessness.

Now changelessness is something the church can offer – in the person of Jesus Christ. The message of the New Testament that Jesus died on the cross, rose from the dead and sent his Holy Spirit into the church on the day of Pentecost – that can be utterly relied on. But the way the church expresses that faith has to change and develop, and some people find that very frightening.

If you often find yourself resisting the principle of discontinuity in your church, it is worth thinking about what causes your fear of change.

### Fear from ignorance

This is something you might call 'first-time fear'. The first time you do anything, you usually feel afraid. I remember my first day at secondary school: everyone seemed six feet tall, I didn't know my way around, and someone told me I was wearing the wrong tie! I can still remember those feelings as if it happened yesterday. We are all afraid

of the unknown, and there are things in church life
we may not be familiar with: new styles of worship,
physical healings or prophecies. As soon as we feel
unsure, the devil races in to develop our fears:
'This is going to split the church', 'People are going
to be offended'.

After many years of praying about the things of
the Holy Spirit, I have come to a profound conclu-
sion: I should actually be more afraid of offending
God than I am of offending other people. I don't
want to offend God by refusing to accept what he
is offering me and my church; I believe God loves
us and wants the best for us, and if we can only
trust him he will uphold and strengthen us through
all the changes and new developments we face.

*Fear from carnality*

Carnality comes from a Latin word meaning 'flesh'.
I'm using it here to mean the earthly attitudes
which are against the Spirit of God. Attitudes which
have at their heart rebellion against and disobedi-
ence to God.

Think back to the story of Adam and Eve in the
garden of Eden. They were enjoying each other's
company and having fun naming the animals –
'Let's call that one an elephant,' Eve said. 'It looks
more like a cat to me,' replied Adam. Then came
the sin – they disobeyed God. When God came to
walk in the garden, they hid. They were afraid of
the presence of God because of their carnality,
their sinfulness. They had deliberately chosen to
turn away from God's will for them.

In the church there are some people who stubbornly refuse to be obedient to God. 'I won't be part of this,' they object. 'I don't want this happening in our church.' Such resistance to the Holy Spirit produces fear, because darkness doesn't want any dealings with light, and if you set yourself against the will of God you are in rebellion against him.

## Fear from insecurity

Too many of us in the church are insecure. We do not feel secure in the love of God, nor in the family of God, nor in the presence of the Holy Spirit. Too many Christians have a massive inferiority complex, rather like Jeremiah: 'Don't send me, I'm too young, I don't know anything about it.' Frankly, God says, 'Rubbish. If I send you you aren't weak, because I give you whatever gifts you need for the service I ask of you.'

Jesus gave his life so that we might live. He endured a brutal death on the cross because of his love for us. How then can we feel inferior? Our gifts may not be the same as the pastor's but that doesn't matter. Each one of us is God's child, and we should feel secure in his love. Our gifts are needed in the family in which he has placed us, and the Holy Spirit is waiting to empower us still further. With such love surrounding us, how can we be afraid of anything that may happen?

## Changing the community

Once we can rid ourselves of our fears and apprehension about the future, we can begin to take a full part in its development. As our churches change and become vibrant with the love of God, we should be able to reach out into the communities that surround us. What changes do we expect to see there?

You may have lived in your community for ten, twenty, thirty years or longer. You may say with confidence that God wants to work in your community, but can you really see it happening? Do you really believe things will change there? That's when we say that fatal phrase, 'Look, let's be realistic.'

Let's *not* be realistic – at least, let's be God's realists, which means being God's visionaries in faith. Can our community be different? Can the schools and social structure of our town be changed? Or do we have to sit back and say, 'We have to accept things as they are'? I think we know enough about the principle of discontinuity to realise that because Jesus is always the same and his power is always the same, we don't have to stay the same.

I long to see the community touched and changed for Jesus Christ, so that Jesus is talked about in the pubs and in the shops and in the streets.

I do believe that God is beginning to move in our country. The media is taking more and more interest in the good news we have to offer, and we should take every opportunity to talk about our Lord. After all, that is where we belong: not cowering inside the church fearful of change, but outside in the community, telling people about Jesus.

At the first Pentecost the disciples were indoors keeping a low profile; after the coming of the Holy Spirit they were empowered to go out into the crowded city streets to preach Christ crucified. Let us pray for the Holy Spirit to fill us and encourage us too, to go out unafraid, to change ourselves, our church, and our community.

# 5

## *Practical Steps to Experiencing God*

We believe that we can be changed by the power of God, and that God wants to come into our lives and transform them to his glory. But how do we get in touch with God's power? How do we reach out and experience God in our everyday lives? Throughout the Bible there are descriptions of encounters with God, but too often we treat reading the Bible as an intellectual exercise – something to be read in isolation from the rest of our lives.

Before I learned to drive I read the Highway Code very thoroughly; I even persuaded my parents to test me on all the details, so I knew what all the signs meant and the extent of all the stopping distances. But my first driving lesson made it all seem almost irrelevant: once behind the wheel of a real car, ten miles an hour seemed like a hundred and fifty. I couldn't believe the speed at which the hedgerows were zooming past, and I couldn't believe that other cars were allowed on the same

road – some of them even travelling in the opposite
direction! It was a revelation of the difference
between reading the theory in a book, and actually
experiencing the reality for yourself.

So what we need when thinking about God is not a
Highway Code to read and learn academically, but a
guide to help us experience the risen Christ, to feel
his touch on our lives and his power to change us.
This is not an exercise we do once and then forget,
but is the constant renewing of our spiritual lives on
a daily basis. Matthew 7 describes four practical
steps to experiencing God.

## Criticism and confession

> Do not judge, or you too will be judged. For in the same
> way as you judge others, you will be judged, and with
> the measure you use, it will be measured to you.
> Why do you look at the speck of sawdust in your
> brother's eye and pay no attention to the plank in your
> own eye? How can you say to your brother, 'Let me take
> the speck out of your eye,' when all the time there is a
> plank in your own eye? You hypocrite, first take the
> plank out of your own eye, and then you will see clearly
> to remove the speck from your brother's eye (Mt 7:1–5).

This first step comes in two parts. To begin with,
Jesus says that in order to experience him in all his
power, we need to be delivered from the critical
spirit which is constantly finding specks in other
people's eyes. It's a serious thought, but Jesus paints
a hilarious picture like a comedy sketch. There's a
man with a tiny speck in his eye, pulling all sorts of

faces in the mirror, trying to get it out. Then up behind him comes another man with a huge log sticking out of his eye, trying to be helpful and poking around the other man's face – he probably can't even find the man's eye, let alone the minute speck in it.

*Accepting others*

Jesus says that the critical spirit which looks at other people and points the finger in judgement, prevents us from meeting him in a new way. We pick up the habit all too easily from the world around us. Every major newspaper has a gossip columnist whose job seems to be excavating mud to throw at public figures, and hoping some of it sticks. In the first chapter of this book, we've seen how successfully Satan's negative kingdom can dominate our thoughts and speech, causing us always to find something to complain about. Sometimes church communities are the worst places for this: other denominations, other individuals and other patterns of worship all come under fire. Why do we find it so hard to accept other people when they do things differently from us?

For some Christians this critical attitude is like a cancer in their spiritual lives: they may have many gifts, great experiences of God, a desire for holiness, but they constantly complain, ridicule and criticise what others are trying to do. They're so busy sorting out everyone else's problems that they aren't looking at what God wants for them. They have logs in their eyes.

*Seeking forgiveness*

The second step is getting rid of the log in our own eye, and that demands confession. Jesus taught us in the Lord's Prayer that he forgives us as we forgive others. If we haven't got a forgiving spirit ourselves, he can't pour his forgiveness into us.

Many people dam up the channel of God's grace so that he can't pour his Spirit into them, because they refuse to forgive someone. It may be a member of their family, or of their church. It may have happened ten years ago. But they're still holding on to that grudge, and because of that, God cannot bless them. Scripture is quite clear about that: a grudging spirit which holds on to malice will not be blessed. If we judge in that way, we are hardening our hearts against others and against God.

We need to examine our own hearts closely. It's too easy to let ourselves off the hook and think of five other people who really should do something about their logs! A friend of mine once preached a really hard-hitting sermon. He looked out at his congregation to see how they were taking it. He could almost see it being passed down the church as everybody was thinking, 'Wow, that's really good for the row behind.' He almost saw the message go out of the door, because no one wanted it: the back row thought it was good for those outside.

We must grapple with what God is saying to us in this passage: we have to confess our critical spirit and be forgiven.

## Honouring God

> Do not give dogs what is sacred; do not throw your
> pearls to pigs. If you do, they may trample them under
> their feet, and then turn and tear you to pieces (Mt 7:6).

This difficult verse suggests that there are times
when it is wrong to talk in public about your Christian faith. There are certain groups of people who
really don't want to listen, but only to ridicule in a
cynical fashion. You would be throwing the good
things of God before people who aren't fit to
appeciate them.

We need to be very careful about this. There have
been times when I've been verbally attacked for my
Christian faith and asked to defend it, but I have
refused to do so. When Jesus was pushed around by
Herod and Pilate, he wouldn't open his mouth: he
wouldn't give them the satisfaction of letting them
mock again. Some people are so wrapped up in
themselves that they aren't prepared to listen, and
you shouldn't waste your breath on them.

This is not just a direction about the best moments
for evangelism, but the second principle for receiving God's blessing. The deeper implication is this:
don't treat holy things lightly.

### Approaching with awe

One of the diseases of contemporary Christianity is
the habit of treating God so casually in prayer that
we relegate him to being just our buddy.

It's right, of course, to be natural with God in
prayer. We don't need to use flowery or old-

fashioned language, as if he was stuck in the seventeenth century. I heard a story the other day about a fellowship in Devon where one man liked to pray about topical things. He would stand up at the prayer meeting on Tuesday nights and say, 'Lord, I don't know if you've read tonight in the *Torquay Gazette*, how such-and-such happened.' Presumably if the Lord hadn't had his paper delivered by eight o'clock, he hadn't seen it! But that man's casual and informal way of talking to God is right: we don't need to put on airs and graces, but just talk to him as our heavenly Father.

However, there is a boundary line which we must not cross, where informality passes into flippancy – flippancy diminishes God in our eyes and makes us even smaller. James Packer, in his book *Knowing God*, says we are pygmy Christians because we have a pygmy God. If we refer to holy things in a careless way, we are robbed of meeting the living God, because we don't really see him as he truly is.

We need a new vision of the God of the Bible. In the Old Testament, God is seen as striding across the mountains in power, clicking his fingers to bring the world into being, riding on the currents of the air, and holding the whole universe in the hollow of his hand. That's the God whom we worship: a holy and marvellous God, a majestic and tremendous God. Too often we don't treat God with the respect and awe he deserves. A half-hearted request for blessing 'OK, Lord, why don't you zap me now?' – will get us nowhere. We aren't even asking the right being, because a god who can be approached like that isn't the real God.

*Celestial slot-machine*

There is another aspect to this matter of holiness: God won't be used by us. The giver comes first, the gifts second; we have to want God for himself, before anything else. Our love for our husbands and wives would be poor and tawdry if we only loved them for what we could get out of them. The marital relationship is not one of demands, not one of 'If you do this then I'll love you', or 'If you behave in this way then I'll love you'. I love my wife for herself, not for what I may get in return.

True love is selfless. We should love God for himself, not for what we can get out of him. Too often God's baptism of power is limited because we come to him wanting to be made happy, wanting gifts and blessings. God's priority for our life is different from ours. We want to be happy, but God wants us to be holy – however, the second includes the first. If we strive for happiness we may succeed in being vaguely amused; if we strive for holiness we will find happiness too.

We can't treat God as a sort of celestial slot machine where we press a button to be blessed by the Spirit, and out comes the gift we've selected. The renewal movement as a whole is a doorway into the majesty of God – not the end, but only the beginning. Whatever we have seen by way of tongues and prophecy and healing is only the start of what God wants to do. He wants to give us himself in all his glory and power, and when that happens all these precious gifts will seem like mere trinkets by comparison. The diamonds have not arrived yet. It's only when we seek God in his holiness and his almighty power that we will receive the spiritual anointing for which we long.

## The power of persistence

> Ask and it will be given unto you; seek and you will find; knock and the door will be opened to you. For everyone who asks receives; he who seeks finds; and to him who knocks, the door will be opened (Mt 7:7–8).

The verbs in this verse are present continuous imperatives. Basically that means that they are commands to keep on doing something. Keep on asking, keep on seeking, keep on knocking. This persistence is the third step.

What happens when we've tried everything and our prayers don't seem to get through? When the sky is like rock and God seems a million miles away?

I think the biblical injunction is this: we must seek and seek, because God teaches us valuable lessons if we will only stick at them and learn them. We've already said that God wants to make us holy: sometimes it's the process of waiting for him to bless us that brings us to that holiness. In the quiet of prayer, in the time of waiting on the Lord, that's when the dross that surrounds our lives is consumed, and pain strips away our selfishness. God is changing us.

We should never be discouraged when we can't seem to break through into God's presence; we should keep on asking. We are being blessed by God even in the process of asking. Many of the great saints of Scripture struggled for years to be the kind of men and women God wanted them to be.

## Meeting God

If ever there was a man in Scripture who utterly smashed the 'easy believe, easy blessing' idea, it was Job. His family was decimated, his crops destroyed, his cattle gone, his health wrecked, yet he stood before Almighty God and said, 'Although he slay me, yet will I trust him.' Job never gave up; he went on and on seeking for the answers to his problems, the answers that would bring him to know God. Job, at the end of the book, is a totally different man from Job at the beginning, because he had been through the fire and met God. Right at the end we find the lovely verse, 'My ears had heard of you but now my eyes have seen you' (Job 42:5). In other words, 'I used to know about God vaguely, but now I know him personally and powerfully.'

Job would never have come to know the true God without that protracted tearing away of all he held most dear. In the end he stood before God naked and unadorned, without wealth, health or family, ready at last to be touched by him. God did bless him, but it was partly in the long waiting, asking, seeking time that the blessing came.

## The discipline of asking

Prayer is work. It takes effort and it takes persistence. When the reluctant judge finally gave justice to the widow, he did so not because he liked her, but because she kept on and on asking him (Lk 18:1–8). That is not to say that God is unjust or reluctant; nor that he responds to nagging (which of us does?). He is not a vicious God playing games with his children, saying, 'I'll wait till you've asked a hundred times and then I'll answer.' Rather, he is waiting to liberate us into wholeness, and working to bring us to the point where we can meet him. Some of us need the discipline of asking to concentrate our minds, to make us realise what we really want and what is really important.

There is a marvellous story in the Old Testament about Jacob wrestling with the angel. He says, 'I will not let you go until you bless me.' We need that kind of holy fanaticism, not to let go of God until he blesses us and pours his power into our lives.

## Good gifts

The final verses are ones of encouragement to us.

> Which of you, if his son asks for bread, will give him a stone? Or if he asks for a fish, will give him a snake? If you, then, though you are evil, know how to give good gifts to your children, how much more will your Father in heaven give good gifts to those who ask him!(Mt 7:9–11)

When children ask their parents for something, the parents usually love to provide for them if they can. Parents get a great deal of happiness from seeing the joy of their children. How many of us can remember asking for things just before Christmas (that is, around July), and coming down on Christmas morning to find that very present waiting for us

– something we had wanted for a long time. Our parents got just as much joy out of that moment as we did.

In the above passage, God is saying, 'Look, you are weak, evil, sinful human beings, yet you love to give. How much more am I like that! I long to give you gifts, more than you long to receive them. I want to bless you more than you long to be blessed.'

This is what all the other steps lead up to: avoiding a critical spirit and asking for forgiveness; confessing what is wrong and forgiving each other; recognising that God is a holy God and must be desired for himself; persevering with a holy tenacity even when the going gets tough, and believing that God is waiting to give us his good gifts. If we follow these steps we open ourselves up to experience God, and enable him to give us those gifts.

For some of us those gifts come sooner, for others later; but the struggle is not worthless, the wait is not wasted time – it is all part of God's economy in bringing us to himself. We must never stop searching and never stop asking until God's power is poured out on us for his honour and glory, so that we may become the people he wants us to be.

# 6

## How to Be a True Worshipper

When we first have an experience of God, our immediate reaction is to worship him – the holy God who has redeemed us through his Son Jesus Christ. Our hearts are full of thankfulness and praise, so that we say with the psalmist, 'Come, let us bow down in worship, let us kneel before the Lord our Maker; for he is our God, and we are the people of his pasture, the flock under his care' (Ps 95:6,7).

The months and the years go by, and the freshness of our worship somehow fades. We attend the same church, sing the same hymns, and even if our prayers are not spoken in the same words, perhaps we express the same sentiments over and over again. God may be doing new work in our lives, renewing us every day, yet Sunday by Sunday we come to church and we feel stale. What is it that spoils our worship and prevents us from turning to God with joy, awe and love?

I waited patiently for the Lord; he turned to me and heard my cry. He lifted me out of the slimy pit, out of the mud and mire; he set my feet on a rock and gave me a firm place to stand. He put a new song in my mouth, a hymn of praise to our God. Many will see and fear and put their trust in the Lord. Blessed is the man who makes the Lord his trust, who does not look to the proud, to those who turn aside to false gods. Many, O Lord my God, are the wonders you have done. The things you planned for us no one can recount to you, were I to speak and tell of them, they would be too many to declare (Ps 40:1–5).

Yet a time is coming and has now come, when the true worshippers will worship the Father in spirit and truth, for they are the kind of worshippers the Father seeks. God is spirit, and his worshippers must worship in spirit and in truth (Jn 4:23,24).

How can we be true worshippers? We need to consider what worship is and how we approach it before we can worship 'in spirit and in truth'.

## A quiet spirit

Corporate worship is important to our Christian lives – so important that it is worth examining our attitude to it. We can't come into a service with our minds full of a thousand things and expect to click automatically into a worshipful attitude. There is work to be done, preparation to be made, before we can participate fully in what is going on. True worship begins before the service starts.

## Punctuality

Of course, there is always the odd occasion when things go wrong: the phone rings just as you are about to go out, or Aunt Esmeralda drops in at five thirty for a cup of tea. We all know that feeling, when we rush in breathlessly at the last minute, thanking God that we didn't have a collision as we screeched round the corner and found a parking place. What happens is that we miss that calming, quiet time when we compose our hearts and our minds for worship. Singing or prayer goes on around us but it may be fifteen minutes or so before we're really able to tune into the spirit of the service and join in.

However, when we are perpetually late for worship, we need to examine our hearts. Are we guilty of treating God casually? We should always be aware of the significance of worship – it is an audience with King Jesus. Unpunctuality suggests that we don't really care how much we miss – let them start without us and we'll join in when we arrive. But we can't just 'join in', something has been lost. Our worship is delayed and impaired. And it isn't just our own worship: the rest of the congregation is interrupted by a late arrival, so everyone is hurt by our attitude.

## Preparation

Being unpunctual sounds like a mere breach of manners, but in actual fact it is stealing time to prepare our hearts for worship.

I'm not suggesting that we all spend hours before the service in silent meditation: many people teach in Sunday School or are involved in other activities, and on Sunday evening we may have spent the day visiting or entertaining family and friends. We may be busy, we may be in a rush – but we should always allow enough time to prepare our hearts to receive God.

I recall a talk given by John Stott, the Anglican teacher and writer, about how to get in contact with God. There were about a hundred students from Spurgeon's College there, and afterwards several of them asked some deep theological questions. Then one man went straight to the heart of the matter and said, 'John, tell us how you pray.'

And he replied, 'Look, it takes me ages to pray. I go into my study and I feel like a blind man groping along a wall, looking for the door. I can spend ten or twenty minutes praying, asking God to be with me, yet I still feel cold and as if he isn't there. Then suddenly I come to the door and it opens, and I can burst through into God's presence. But it takes time to find it.'

I found that tremendously helpful, because we need to know that prayer takes time. So often we come to prayer with our minds cluttered with everyday concerns, and we can't hear what God is saying to us because of the jangling noise of daily life. That's when we need to take time – a few minutes or even a few seconds – to say, 'Lord, quieten my heart, still my spirit, so I can hear your voice.'

The key to worship is putting our minds under God's control. Only he can quieten our spirits so that we can turn to him and hear him.

Once we have calmed our thoughts so that we are

absorbed in God rather than in our daily business, we need to spend some time in confession. When we look at our lives in the light of God's holiness, even the best of us look rather shabby. We retreat into the carnal very easily: we snap at our wife or shout at the children, we come to church with a critical spirit about others, and suddenly we are drifting away from God's way into sin. That sin obscures our view of God just as our busyness stops our ears to his voice, so we need to start again, confessing our sin and asking God to make us clean.

Punctuality and preparation are the keys to the quiet spirit which is ready to accept God's grace.

## A real relationship

Recently my house has been visited by some miracle workers: two men who are particularly gifted in practical things. They snap their fingers and cupboards and shelves appear, electrical points emerge from the walls as if by magic, and a whole loft can be converted into a study with seemingly no effort. After a while I began to feel a little inferior, and I wondered if my wife was thinking, 'How come I didn't get a husband like that?'

Fortunately, the quality of our marriage doesn't depend on my performance in DIY, or indeed in any one area. Our marriage is based on a relationship, and because of that it survives and grows, even though I don't always fix things when I'm asked.

In just the same way, the quality of worship depends on our relationship with God, not on our performance in church or anywhere else.

What goes on in church isn't a performance. The congregation is not putting on a show for God. The singing doesn't have to be like a professional concert, and the speaking doesn't have to be like a theatrical performance. God isn't interested in performances. We should try to do everything as well as we can because we are doing something for God, but unless our relationship with God is right it all counts for nothing.

Nor is the congregation an audience with the minister up front putting on a show, with God as prompter.

Basically, our worship is as good as our relationship with God. What we are saying is, 'Lord, you matter to us. We are coming into your presence to offer you praise.' It has to be a real relationship before it can be real worship.

## Truth not taste

Far too often we make decisions about worship on the grounds of what we feel we might enjoy, which is really a question of taste. We might wonder which two songs God likes most – 'Thine be the glory, risen, conquering Son', or 'O Lamb of God you take away our sin'. In actual fact God doesn't like either of them especially. He isn't interested in the things we do in worship; he is interested in worshippers. He likes those two songs in the proportion in which we worship him in them. He loves any song if our hearts are filled with worship because we are reaching out to him 'in spirit and in truth'.

The issue here is truth, not taste. It doesn't matter

which songs we prefer or which phrases we use in prayer, or whether our tastes coincide with those of the rest of the congregation. What matters is whether God receives worship. It doesn't matter whether some people raise their arms in praise as they sing: some people do this because they are genuinely moved, others do it because the person next to them is doing it and they don't want anyone thinking they're unspiritual.

Songs will change and be forgotten. God will raise up a new generation of songmakers in the future. What matters is not what we get out of worship, or whether we are enjoying ourselves or not, but whether we are reaching out to the true God in love.

## An act of will

Have you ever noticed how many times Scripture includes the word 'will' when talking about worship? 'I will extol the Lord at all times; his praise will be always on my lips. My soul will boast in the Lord' (Ps 34:1–2). 'I will praise God's name in song and glorify him in thanksgiving' (Ps 69:30).

There are times when we feel we can't worship because our emotions are not free to do so. We have had a bad week because we've been under a lot of pressure, we argue with the family in the car on the way to church, and when we arrive we think, 'I can't worship properly this morning, I'm just not in the mood.' We can't afford to have our worship directed solely by our emotions. We praise God because he deserves it, not because we feel like it. Worship is primarily an act of the will. If we only worshipped

God when we felt like it, how often would he be worshipped?

Worship as an act of the will doesn't mean that it will be cold and clinical; rather the opposite. It's when our worship is directed by our emotions that it is shallow and superficial: one week we feel high and have a really enjoyable time, the next week we feel low and the worship feels bad. But if our worship is based on our will, God can take that will and pour his emotion into it; in that way we will find true joy, true excitement, true love for him.

We praise God because he is worthy to be praised. Jesus died for us; he gave his life for us; he gave us the Holy Spirit – that is truth and it will never change. We may feel horrible and we may not feel like saying it, but that doesn't change the facts at all. What God can do is to bring our emotions in line with the facts, so that we rejoice to proclaim his salvation. The facts of Jesus' resurrection, the gift of the Holy Spirit, and of eternal life should fill us with joy. But because of the Fall our emotions are twisted – they don't always respond as they should. In heaven our emotions will be restored to perfection, so that we will respond with perfect joy and love to the facts of our redemption.

Meanwhile it is up to us: if we make an act of will, coming to worship humbly, God will give our feelings a helping hand.

## Travelling together

In almost every church, the worship is structured. In churches where a liturgy is used, the framework and much of the detail is given – the words of the responses and prayers and so on – but the individual minister is still free to plan the tone of the service every week. In churches where there is no liturgy there is still generally some overall plan, whatever the theme or the season of the year.

In my own church, we usually begin with a hymn or song which states an objective truth, not a reflective worship song. This is because when people are gathered together from their various homes and backgrounds, they need to establish a common starting-point, a shared truth about God. Then we move on through Scripture readings and other songs towards worship. It's a kind of progression from the objective to the subjective; from the declaration of fact to the spiritual perception of God; from theology to experience.

It was at the Bethany Fellowship, founded by Colin Urquhart, that I first heard the illustration of the plane journey as a way of thinking about the way a worship service flows and develops.

All the people travelling from a certain airport come into the lounge, with tickets, baggage, families and friends. It's chaos. Then they go through the passport check and into the international lounge where it's much quieter. When they get on the aircraft itself things are even more orderly because they are all going to the same destination. Then the plane taxis onto the runway, speeds up and finally takes off into the air, up through the clouds and into the sunlight.

Our services start with similar chaos as we gather together from all directions, with our parking

problems and the children and our books and
notices. Then we move a little closer to the worship
as things get sorted out, the children go to their classes, and we have time to settle in and prepare ourselves. At last we're called by the flight attendant and
find ourselves in our seats and ready for take-off.

That is the point at which we remind ourselves of
the facts of the Gospel, just as we remember the facts
about flight as the aircraft taxis along the runway:
the plane may be massive, but it has the power to get
off the ground. But once we have taken off into the
sunlight, those facts fade into the background as we
experience the excitement of actually flying. Similarly, we state the facts of our faith at the beginning
of the service, and then we take off into worship: the
facts stay the same but we have gone beyond the
reach of theology and words about God. We have
taken off into experiencing him.

If we understand that development, we can help
to create the momentum which makes it possible.
The Spirit can provide the power to lift us up, to
move us on from theology to experience, to release
us into true worship.


## Governed by the Spirit

The next stage in our worship is to let the Spirit take
control. We must constantly tune in to God, asking
him to speak to us, to challenge, bless, direct or
change us. Sometimes God wants to show us a sin we
were unaware of; sometimes he wants to speak to
the whole congregation; sometimes he wants to tell
us whom to speak to, or put a picture in our minds

of something we can do. But we must be reaching out to God before we can receive his word.

It isn't easy to learn to focus on God in this way, for we need to bring our thoughts under his discipline before our spirits move closer to him. Those who have the gift of tongues may have an advantage here, as they can use it as a channel to direct their thoughts to God – provided, of course, that their use of it doesn't distract others near them. The use of that gift can open the floodgates of blessing, but it is perfectly possible for others who don't have that gift to worship in the spirit equally well. We must be open to God so that he can speak to us as he chooses.

Being as open as this can make us feel very vulnerable, and people often become alarmed when we talk about the spiritual nature of worship. But worship is, obviously, not like singing with the crowd at the local. We are meeting with God, and when worship moves into the spiritual realms, nothing else and no one else matters. We can trust God.

The Bible says that things should be done decently and in order, so when we allow the Spirit to take over and govern our worship, we can be assured that things are not going to get out of control. Worship with the Spirit in control is in God's hands, and what could be safer than that?

God wants us to relax in his presence and trust in his fatherly love; he wants to give us freedom in worship. For some that may mean dancing around with their arms in the air; for others it may mean sitting quietly in God's presence. But worship governed by the Spirit is true worship.

## Working at worship

All this is hard work: it's hard to concentrate on God, to focus on him, and to bring yourself in obedience under his will. You may confidently expect to go home after worship feeling tired, as well as refreshed! Some people come to worship with the spectator mentality, hoping that the minister will generate enough enthusiasm to make the service work. But you can't just come along and expect it to happen to you. You must willingly commit yourself to worship God. The great calls to worship of the ancient church proclaimed, 'Let us come together to praise him.' Worship is something we do together, not something we passively receive.

## The power to heal

When we finally arrive at this experience of worship, 'in spirit and in truth', we will discover some important facts. First, worship is powerful. In my own church, more people appear to come to Christ through the experience of worship than through the preaching. This is not because the preaching of the word is unimportant, but because the worship softens their hearts so that they are receptive to the word. Often when people tell me how much they have been helped by a particular service, I think they're going to thank me for some telling point I made in the sermon, but almost always they say, 'There was a tremendous sense of God's presence in the worship.'

In fact, there are occasions when we hardly need

to preach at all. I remember one Sunday in my home church when I was very young, when a woman got up from her seat and walked down to the front of the church and knelt. The service had only just started, and the preacher went over to speak to her quietly. She said that she had come to know Christ in that service. God had done what he intended to do in her life, without the aid of a preacher!

Worship is also cleansing. We confess our sins at the beginning of the service, when we are preparing ourselves, but as we progress, true worship brings us into the presence of the living God, and that is a humbling experience. We see ourselves as we really are, and that is cleansing: true worship disinfects our egotism.

Finally, worship is healing. We can feel God's healing touch not just by having hands laid on us, but when we remain in our seats, singing or praying or in silence. We can be healed physically, emotionally and spiritually as we are bathed in the love of God.

Worship is all these things, because it puts us in a special relationship with God. The psalmist says, 'He inhabits the praises of his people' – when we praise him he dwells here among us, in all his power and his glory. Worship is the opportunity for the Holy Spirit to touch every heart, bringing us closer to him, and making us the spiritual, truthful, worshipping church he wants us to be.

# 7

## *Forgiveness and Acceptance*

As Christians we are generally very bad at receiving what God wants to give us: either we can't believe God's gifts are really being offered to us, or we don't know how to accept them. This is especially serious in one crucial area – that of forgiveness. In the last chapter we talked about preparing our hearts for worship, and confessing our faults so that we can turn afresh to God, cleansed and healed. Even when we have made our commitment to Christ and been forgiven, we don't become perfect overnight: we go on failing and sinning, and so we go on needing God's forgiveness every day. Yet we often find it difficult to believe that we can really be forgiven, because we fail to understand the basic principles of God's forgiveness.

### Understanding forgiveness

There are three fundamental ideas which we must

grasp if we wish to understand how to accept God's forgiveness, and they are all outlined for us in Scripture.

### Earnestly desired

First, we have the parable of the Pharisee and the tax collector (Lk 18:13). Some of us may have fallen into the trap of feeling spiritual and praying, 'I thank you, Lord, that I'm a member of this church, and that I'm really growing fast in my spiritual life. I thank you that you accept me now because I'm obeying you and witnessing to you.' We probably wouldn't have thought much of the other fellow who prayed, 'Lord, I don't go to church, and I don't know much about Christianity, and I'm a bit pathetic but I ask you to forgive me because I desperately need it.'

In the parable, the man whose prayer was answered was the one who really wanted to be forgiven. One of our major problems is complacency: we aren't sure that we actually need to be forgiven that much.

This is a major stumbling-block for many non-Christians. They find it hard to believe that they need to repent ('I'm a good, moral, upright citizen – I've never killed anybody') because they have never looked at themselves in the light of God's holiness. Yet once we have made that first, difficult step, and realised how much we need God's forgiveness, and turned our lives over to him, we go on making the same mistake. After all, we're so much better than we used to be – there just isn't so much to forgive any more – is there?

In fact, once the searching light of God's love is shining in our lives, we should see more and more clearly how much we need to change, and how much we need to submit to the guidance of the Holy Spirit. We should be longing to be made clean, to come nearer to the pattern of Jesus Christ.

When people came to Jesus for healing, he would say, 'What do you want me to do for you?' They didn't reply, 'Well, how about ten minutes of your time and a brief discussion on the finer points of the law?' Rather, they said, 'I want to receive my sight.' And Jesus acted in response to that urgent desire for healing. This picks up the psalmist's idea: 'Delight yourself in the Lord and he will give you the desires of your heart' (Ps 37:4).

A casual approach to God means that we don't really believe in the seriousness of sin, or in the holiness of God. We must earnestly desire to be forgiven – then we can receive the gift of forgiveness.

*Freely given*

'Whoever is thirsty, let him come; and whoever wishes, let him take the free gift of the water of life' (Rev 23:17). 'The gift of God is eternal life' (Rom 6:23).

Many of us find it hard to accept that forgiveness, eternal life and love are all free gifts from God. Deep down, we don't want to receive charity, a hand-out; we would feel much happier if there was something we had to do to earn these things – something other, that is, than reach out and accept them from God's hand.

The hymn 'Rock of ages' has some helpful

comments on this problem. Verse two reads:

> Not the labours of my hands
> Can fulfil thy law's demands;
> Could my zeal no respite know,
> Could my tears for ever flow,
> All for sin could not atone,
> Thou must save, and thou alone.

Even people who have received salvation by faith want to earn merit with God as they go along, as if God were in the business of counting up spiritual Brownie points. But we cannot earn forgiveness: it's a marvellous free gift. Until we can rid ourselves of the idea that there are strings attached, we cannot fully accept that gift. It doesn't cost anything at all to be forgiven – just your whole life. We can think through the implications of that for ever!

### Instantly received

The other principle of forgiveness is that it is a reality now, at this moment, not when we have fulfilled any conditions or performed any tasks. This is what God is like, and the God of the Old Testament is unchanged today.    Isaiah 42 tells how the nation of Israel turned away from God and became desperately corrupt. Then come the first two words of Chapter 43: 'But now.' A kind of divine imperative sweeps into the situation, declaring that all that is past. God is ready to forgive this minute and move into your life now: 'Fear not, for I have redeemed you; I have summoned you by name; you are mine' (Is 43:1).

In the same way, Paul, writing to the Corinthians, says, 'I tell you, now is the time of God's favour, now is the day of salvation' (2 Cor 6:2). God's salvation is immediate.

Of course, what we would really like is to go on atoning for our sins for a while until we somehow feel we've become righteous enough to earn salvation – back to the old refusal to accept a gift freely given. We feel we ought to suffer a bit longer before God can really forgive us, because we grow up with a kind of punishment-precedes-forgiveness understanding.

When I was young I was sometimes sent to my room when I'd been naughty. 'Go to your room,' my father would say, 'and when you've thought about this enough you may come down.' I never knew what 'enough' was or how long it was supposed to take; I just waited long enough for the storm to die out downstairs and then reappeared as if I'd earned the right to come back into civilised society.

That's the kind of thinking that underlies our reluctance to receive forgiveness now. But we don't need to hide away from God's love any longer: he is ready to receive us now.

### Erecting barriers

Even when we understand these aspects of God's forgiveness, we still fail to accept it, for a variety of reasons. We erect barriers that prevent God's love reaching us: the first two barriers contradict one another (but we are contradictory people).

*Unworthiness*

The story of the prodigal son is a classic example of this barrier. Sitting in the pigsty, starving and ragged, the prodigal son came to the point of saying, 'I could go home, but I'm not worthy to receive my father's forgiveness.' He had, after all, treated his father pretty shabbily – suggesting that he really couldn't wait for him to die, and asking for his share of the money now; then going off and spending it all, and then coming back and asking for charity. Yet his father received him back with love and honour, heaped good things on him, and rejoiced.

The reason for this reception is crucial: it was not based on the worthiness of the son, but on the love of the father. And our relationship with God is not based on our worthiness or our treatment of him, but on his love for us.

Many people suffer so badly from guilt and lack of self-esteem that it ruins the way they relate to other people and the way they relate to God. They feel that they have failed and been forgiven a hundred times, yet they are still making a mess of things – why should God bother with them any longer? In one way, they are absolutely right – there's no earthly reason why God should receive us, but a heavenly one, because God loves us as we are.

This idea is life-giving in its release: God loves us where we are, unworthy as we are. He doesn't love us because of what we may be tomorrow or next week when we've conquered that sin or this problem – he loves us now, just as we are: unspiritual, with feeble quiet times and sporadic church attendance and besetting sins. And he waits to forgive us and bless us now, because of that love.

## Pride

The opposite error to the above is pride: back to the Pharisee in the temple. We don't always realise that we have anything to be forgiven. In 1 Corinthians 5 Paul rebukes the church for sexual sin. The people should have been very disturbed about it, but they weren't. They couldn't see what was wrong, or what needed forgiveness.

Perhaps fewer Christians suffer from pride than from the feeling of unworthiness, but it is still common. Some people feel that they are fairly good Christians, but are completely oblivious to the maelstrom of bad relationships that surrounds them, the family and friends whom they hurt daily by their words and actions. Some of us are guilty of not receiving forgiveness because we don't believe there's much wrong in our lives.

## Unbelief

The third barrier is unbelief. 'See to it, brothers, that none of you has a sinful, unbelieving heart that turns away from the living God' (Heb 3:12).

In the Anglican liturgy the sentence is repeated every Sunday: 'I believe in the forgiveness of sins.' We all, from whatever church tradition, share that belief. Yet the step from belief to experience is one we refuse to make. We may claim all the right things, say all the right words, yet fail to make it correspondingly real in our own lives. We're great at talking about the Christian life on Sunday, yet we can't bring the reality into our workplace on Monday. We don't really believe in a practical way, and so we turn our hearts away from the living God.

## Seeing results

Once we have understood these principles and broken down these barriers, we open ourselves up to receiving God's forgiveness. Over and over again as I counsel people, I see them reach out to God in humility and repentance. As they accept God's forgiveness in even a small measure, they are changed in great measure.

## Blessing

'Repent and be baptised, every one of you, in the name of Jesus Christ for the forgiveness of sins. And you will receive the gift of the Holy Spirit' (Acts 2:38). This is a clear biblical demonstration that forgiveness precedes a spiritual blessing – in this case the gift of the Holy Spirit. And that principle, which is true at the new birth, is true throughout the Christian life. When we ask for forgiveness and receive it, we are cleansed. God can pour his love and blessings into us. God isn't waiting for us to become perfect; he's just waiting for us to accept his forgiveness. When we do so, there's a tremendous sense of release as our burdens are lifted and we feel his presence.

## Healing

Isaiah 53:5 shows us that healing is rooted in the cross: 'By his wounds we are healed.' The link between healing and forgiveness emerges again in

Mark 2 when the paralysed man is let down through the roof by his friends. Jesus said to him, 'Your sins are forgiven.' You can just imagine all the teachers of the law saying, 'What's going on here?' Jesus' response is: 'Which is easier, forgiving sins or healing the body? I'll show you the first is true by doing the second.' And the paralysed man gets up and walks off with his bed rolled up under his arm.

It's perhaps only in recent years that medical science has begun to rediscover the link between emotional and spiritual tensions and the ills of the body. When the doctor can't find a cause for your headache or backache, he may well put it down to stress. Over a long period, stress can produce severe physical symptoms. I think there's no doubt that some of us are physically ill because we are not forgiven; some of us think we have a mental or emotional problem when we really need to receive forgiveness from God.

To return to the words of 'Rock of ages':

Nothing in my hand I bring,
Simply to thy cross I cling;
Naked, come to thee for dress;
Helpless, look to thee for grace;
Foul, I to the fountain fly;
Wash me, Saviour, or I die.

## Forgiving others

In the Sermon on the Mount, Jesus taught: 'If you forgive men when they sin against you, your heavenly Father will also forgive you. But if you do not forgive men their sins, your Father will not forgive you' (Mt 6:14–15).

He didn't say, 'I've forgiven you, and now that you're feeling really spiritual, why don't you consider forgiving a few other people?' Rather, he said, 'The foundation of my forgiveness to you is the reciprocal forgiving of others. You must forgive other people.' This is a divine command, and we need to consider the implications for us, both within the church fellowship and in the wider world.

## Divided society

We live in a society where division and lack of acceptance is rife. Not only is there racial division between black and white, but within the sub-groups of black and white there are areas of great antagonism. There is a lack of acceptance between the generations, between the North and the South, between the affluent and the poor, and so on.

These kinds of divisions are in a sense self-perpetuating: any group which excludes us makes us feel insecure, so we cling all the more closely to whatever group we feel we belong to. We may even criticise or ridicule other groups for their traditions, ways of dress, or manner of speech.

Ultimately what we all want is to be accepted, by our peer group, by our church family, by our friends. Acceptance is very important to us: so much so that it often produces these antagonistic patterns of behaviour towards those who do not conform to our ideas – hardly a sign of love and acceptance and forgiveness.

## Accepted by God

'Accept one another, then, just as Christ accepted you, in order to bring praise to God' (Rom 15:7).

These are the words which bring us release from insecurity and antagonism towards others: Christ has accepted us. Whatever our background, class, colour or intellect, Jesus Christ, through his death, has reached out to us with his divine hands to hold us safe. There is no sin so terrible that we cannot be accepted, no secret hidden in our past so bad that we cannot come to him with confidence. God loves us enough to accept us just as we are – but he loves us too much to leave us the way we are! So he will cleanse us and change us and draw us closer to him day by day.

In fact, it's often not sin which keeps us away from God as much as emotional damage. The accumulated hurts of a lifetime of small rejections make us unwilling to risk opening our hearts to love. Yet God is waiting to heal those wounds too. The great and glorious truth of the Christian gospel is that no one is excluded from the arms of Jesus Christ: he longs for the hurt and the injured and the sinful to come to him for forgiveness and healing.

## Reaching out

But even as we are caught up in the joy of the realisation that God loves and accepts us, we must hear the echo of Scripture: 'Accept one another...as Christ accepted you'; 'Forgive us...as we have forgiven'. If it is true that God has accepted us, then we must accept one another in the name of Christ. How terrible to be accepted by God, only to repay that love by rejecting someone else for whom Christ has died.

Jesus told the story of the unforgiving servant to illustrate how wrong such behaviour is. The king releases one man from his debt, even though he owes an impossibly large amount of money. That same man immediately goes off and throws another into the debtors' prison, for a much smaller debt. It's an example of how a man who receives grace from God can refuse to offer grace to others.

We have been forgiven so much; we have been granted so great an acceptance; how can we then continue with our petty quarrels, our idle criticisms, and our trivial gossip? God accepts us as we are, and we are called on to exercise the same acceptance. We need to reach out to others in love, to show God's love within the fellowship and to the outside world 'in order to bring praise to God'. Then we will fully understand the meaning of God's forgiveness, and glorify him for it.

# 8

## *The Unfair Love of God*

God forgives us because he loves us. And if recognising God's forgiveness calls us to forgive others, so recognising God's love has implications too.

### The principle of fairness

I have three children, and of course, as any parent knows, that makes me an expert on fairness. Their perpetual complaint is 'It's not fair' – about everything from who needs new shoes to who has the biggest apple. I can still remember my mother dealing with me and my sisters at mealtimes by counting out the chips! Children have a very strong concept of fairness; it seems to be built into their perception of the world right from the start. They want things to be fair and they want their fair share of everything: your money, your time, your love.

## Human justice

Our adult lives are characterised by the same attitude to justice. We want our rights, we want what we deserve, we want to be dealt with in a just way.

As a result of this, our society is threaded through with the principle of negotiated fairness. Wage settlements are arranged on the basis of compromise: employees demand one thing, employers offer another, and in the end they usually settle on the middle ground, agreed to be a fair wage for a fair amount of work.

The legal profession gets most of its work from the attempt to ensure fairness between two parties in dispute, whether it's over the ownership of a piece of land or the settlement of money. In divorce proceedings a court has to determine the fair distribution of responsibility between partners, for providing money and care for the children and keeping a home going.

The principle of fairness underlies all the contracts and bargains and interactions in our society: it seems like a good principle. Yet when we turn to the heart of the Christian message we find an apparent opposite to this principle: the gospel has some aspects which are fundamentally unfair, and that is what makes it such a miraculous authority and power.

## Heavenly love

We want justice, or at least we claim to. If we knew what we really deserved, in spiritual terms, we probably wouldn't be so keen. Fortunately for us, at the heart of the Christian gospel is a message of unfairness: that is, that God loves us without conditions, without negotiation, without the need for us to contribute anything to the bargain.

It is difficult for us to grasp that God's love is not fair. If it were fair, we would be loved as much as we deserved. If we had a good week with the Lord, if we behaved ourselves and read the Bible and prayed a lot, then God would love us a lot by Sunday. If we forgot to read our Bible and overslept our prayer time and were grumpy with the family all week, he wouldn't love us so much – we hadn't kept our side of the bargain.

But God's love isn't like that; it isn't based on fairness at all, because it is unconditional love. God is committed to us by the covenant of the cross of Jesus Christ, and that is a miracle we can hardly accept.

What do I have to do to become a Christian? Most people find it a problem that they don't have to do anything to earn Christian faith – they don't have to be better behaved, chalk up a lot of good works, or fulfil any conditions. Nothing is required from us in order for God's love to be revealed in our lives; simply faith in what he has already done.

Naturally, when we sin we feel far from God; but God doesn't love us one scrap less when we sin than when we don't. When we come into a relationship with Jesus Christ, we make a covenant. Because of that covenant God promises to love us, for Jesus' sake, whatever we're like. We can come to worship in the confidence that God doesn't love us any the less.

Some people ask whether that isn't just an excuse for being as sinful as we like, if we're sure God will keep on loving us. But of course, if we have thankful hearts for what Jesus has done in redeeming us, we don't want to feel distant from God. If we are rebellious and sinful, we know we feel the results in our own life: we lose the power of the Spirit, we lose joy in worship, we lose the close contact with God that enables us to pray in his will and see answers to prayer. But those are the effects of us moving away from God, not of him moving away from us. His love does not change.

## Who is my neighbour?

On one occasion an expert in the law stood up to test Jesus. 'Teacher,' he asked, 'what must I do to inherit eternal life?'

'What is written in the law?' he replied. 'How do you read it?'

He answered, '"Love the Lord your God with all your heart and with all your soul and with all your strength and with all your mind"; and, "Love your neighbour as yourself".'

'You have answered correctly,' Jesus replied. 'Do this and you will live.'

But he wanted to justify himself, so he asked Jesus, 'And who is my neighbour?'

In reply Jesus said: 'A man was going down from Jerusalem to Jericho, when he fell into the hands of robbers. They stripped him of his clothes, beat him and went away, leaving him half dead. A priest happened to be going down the same road, and when he saw the man, he passed by on the other side. So, too, a Levite, when he came to the place and saw him, passed by on the other side. But a Samaritan, as he travelled, came where the man was; and when he saw him, he took pity on him. He went to him and bandaged his wounds, pouring on oil and wine. Then he put the man on his own donkey, brought him to an inn and took care of him. The next day he took out two silver coins and gave them to the innkeeper. "Look after him," he said, "and when I return, I will reimburse you for any extra expense you may have."

'Which of these three do you think was a neighbour to the man who fell into the hands of robbers?'

The expert in the law replied, 'The one who had mercy on him.' Jesus told him, 'Go and do likewise' (Lk 10:25–37).

*Ancient outcast*

The Jews hated the Gentiles: one ancient rabbi said that God only created the Gentiles to fuel the fires of hell. However, the one group they hated more than the Gentiles was the Samaritans. They were linked with the Jews historically through Abraham, Jacob and Esau, but they were suspected because of their mixed ancestry. They also shared some beliefs with the Jews, and their Holy Book contained the Law but not the Prophets. But the real contention was the fact that the Samaritans had their own temple on Mount Gerizim and did not recognise the Temple at Jerusalem. They were considered traitors to the faith. The Jews regarded them with a sort of religious hatred with some racial antagonism thrown in.

The Samaritans didn't have much time for the Jews either: they thought they were a stuck-up bunch of religious prigs – and that was on a good day. Geographically they were neighbours, but they had nothing else in common.

Now, if the principle of justice had operated in the case of the man who fell into the hands of robbers, it would have ruined the story. The other two characters had their own good reasons for ignoring the casualty by the side of the road: if he was dead, the priest and the Levite would have defiled themselves by touching him, and been unable to fulfil their priestly duties or any other business at the Temple. The Samaritan had good reason too: he owed nothing to any Jew; no Jew would have eaten a meal with him, or even spoken to him if it could be avoided. Why should he go out of his way to help someone who doubtless would have despised him? The principle of justice dictated that the Samaritan, too, should walk by on the other side of the road.

What Jesus is illustrating here is a love that goes beyond fairness, the unconditional love that enables us to love God with all our heart, soul, mind and strength, and our neighbour as ourself (Lk 10:27–28). Jesus is saying that our neighbour isn't someone who is linked to us racially, or by friendship, or shared interests or shared beliefs. He just happens to be there – living next door, or passing by, or standing next to us in a crowd.

### Today's outsider

We may offer help to our friends willingly and lovingly, but when it comes to people we don't know, our principles fall apart a little. On the whole we reserve our love for those who are familiar, the people who look and act like us, with whom we feel safe. When we are faced with someone of a different race, or different appearance, we feel afraid and unsure: suddenly that love for our neighbour becomes very hard to express.

Some time ago I was in a busy shopping centre, pushing my younger daughter in her buggy. It started to rain heavily so we stopped under a shop awning to shelter, along with quite a number of other people. Suddenly a man appeared on the pavement, swinging his umbrella, and singing to all the passers-by. Everybody looked very embarrassed; no one wanted to walk past him to get under the shelter any more, and those already there edged away to the sides, as far from him as they could get. They even looked away so they didn't have to meet his eye, in case he spoke to them.

After a while he came over and sang to us, so I knelt down and said to Cara, 'Let's listen to what this man has to sing.' He asked if he could sing to Cara, and I said, 'Of course.'

He stroked her cheek and sang a song, and at the end he said, 'That was Nat King Cole.'

'That was very nice,' I answered.

'Do you want another?'

'Sure,' I said, and he started singing again.

As this conversation flourished I noticed the crowd had relaxed; they were watching now and moving nearer, because it no longer seemed a threatening situation, once we were talking. The lunatic doing his own thing in the rain in the middle of the High Street was actually a perfectly harmless old man – and Cara was too young to know the difference anyway. Yet normally civil, sensible people had turned their backs on him because they were afraid.

We'd much rather love the people who are easy to relate to: it's harder to love the stranger, the outsider and the outcast.

## Channels for love

The whole of Scripture challenges our conception of what love means. It's not just about loving the safe, familiar, likeable people. It's not the sort of love which is conditional on certain kinds of behaviour. God's love isn't like that, and we are called to love as God loves us.

### Conditional love

The problem we have in expressing God's love is one reason why Christianity fails to make the impact on the world that it should.

In our marriages – the one place where it should be easy to express love – we often behave in a carnal way. We offer physical or friendship love rather than dynamic, unconditional love. The better our spouse 'behaves', the more willing we are to show our love. We slide into moods where we withhold love – we are silent or uncommunicative or grumpy – until our partner recognises that we have been offended in some way, and apologises or makes amends. The unspoken statement is that as long as our partners meet certain requirements, we will go on loving them.

In our churches we receive people with conditional love: they can be part of our fellowship if they

dress like us and behave like us, if they think and
speak like us. Otherwise they are sure to feel 'an outsider'. Or we check out the other members of our
housegroups in the light of our own arrogance. Are
they sound; do they worship in the way we worship,
think in the way we think, use the same words that
we use? When they do, we open our hearts to them,
but until then we hold something back.

In our families we find it hard to love uncondi-
tionally, because we punish our children by our
anger. When they do something which annoys us,
it's too easy to make them feel rejected, pushed out
from the circle of our love.

### Christian love

This conditional love is not what we are called to
demonstrate to the world. God's love for us is
unconditional, because 'while we were still sinners,
Christ died for us' (Rom 5:8). He didn't wait until we
were perfect or even half approaching it, because
out of his grace he decided to love us as we are.

In the Old Testament that unconditional love is
called covenant love. It describes the relationship
between two people who have a contractual obliga-
tion. In the New Testament it is called *agape*, the
supernatural love given by God himself. This means
that the full picture, as revealed in the Old and the
New Testaments, shows love flowing vertically from
God to us, and then horizontally from us to our fellow men, our neighbours. We are to be channels for
God's unconditional love to flow out to everyone
around us.

This means that in our marriages we shouldn't

pay one another back for the things we do wrong. When I forget for the hundredth time to tell my wife about a meeting which I didn't write in the diary, she doesn't say, 'Well, the fairest thing is that you cancel that meeting,' or, 'I think you ought to be extra nice to me to make up.' I know I've got it wrong again, but our love for one another is unconditional – that's marriage at its best.

In Ephesians 5:25 Paul says, 'Husbands, love your wives, just as Christ loved the church.' Husbands are to be channels through which the unconditional love of Christ flows through to their wives.

Unconditional love means that in our church fellowships we stop having a mental checklist of requirements for acceptable members, but reach out willingly to offer friendship to everyone.

It means that with our children we stop confusing unconditional love with uncritical love. Loving our children doesn't mean condoning their sins and ignoring their errors. As parents we have a duty to guide our children and discipline them if we want them to grow up in the security of God's will, but we don't retract our love from them. We should reject their behaviour, not them.

It means that in our friendships outside the church we don't get in a huff with people or cross them off our Christmas card list because we don't quite see eye to eye with them any more. We cannot retreat behind some pseudo-spiritual gobbledegook, and say that of course we love everybody, if in our hearts we are harbouring the sort of resentment which cuts us off from people. Hurts and irritations have to be reconciled so that we are free to be channels of the unconditional love of God.

Sometimes we need to come to the point in our lives where all our hurts and resentments are drowned in the vast ocean of God's love for us. Maybe we haven't been treated fairly by life, but let us give thanks that we aren't treated fairly by God, either. For we don't deserve our salvation, we receive it through God's grace and goodness.

We have to reject the temptation to respond to unfair treatment with bitterness. Guided by the unfair love of God, we should respond to everyone – family, friends, strangers, neighbours – with the kind of love with which God has loved us.

# 9

## *The Writing on the Wall*

We use the phrase 'The writing on the wall' to mean that the day of judgement is not far off. It's not an example of ancient graffiti or the story of an aerosol artist; it indicates that everything is decided, or that trouble is looming for someone – as it certainly was for King Belshazzar.

King Belshazzar gave a great banquet for a thousand of his nobles and drank wine with them. While Belshazzar was drinking his wine, he gave orders to bring in the gold and silver goblets that Nebuchadnezzar his father had taken from the temple in Jerusalem, so that the king and his nobles, his wives and his concubines might drink from them. So they brought in the gold goblets that had been taken from the temple of God in Jerusalem, and the king and his nobles, his wives and his concubines drank from them. As they drank the wine, they praised the gods of gold and silver, of bronze, iron, wood and stone.

Suddenly the fingers of a human hand appeared and

wrote on the plaster of the wall, near the lampstand in
the royal palace. The king watched the hand as it wrote.
His face turned pale and he was so frightened that his
knees knocked together and his legs gave way (Dan
5:1–6).

King Belshazzar was giving a great feast for his
nobles. He invited them to drink with him, and
then remembered that his father had looted
some particularly fine goblets on one of his
conquests. They happened to come from the
temple in Jerusalem, but this did not bother
King Belshazzar in the slightest. While they used
them, they sang songs of praise to their own
gods – gods made out of wood and metal.

There was a limit to what God would take.
The hand appeared and wrote on the wall, and
it had a devastating effect on Belshazzar – he
was terrified out of his wits by this supernatural
demonstration that God was angry with him.

The words were *Mene, mene, tekel, parsin*. Later
in the chapter they were explained by Daniel:
'God has numbered the days of your reign and
brought it to an end...You have been weighed
in the scales and found wanting...Your kingdom
is divided and given to the Medes and the Per-
sians' (Dan 5:26). In verse 30 we read: 'That very
night Belshazzar, king of the Babylonians, was
slain, and Darius the Mede took over the kingdom, at the age of sixty-two.' Sir William Walton
wrote the piece of music 'Belshazzar's Feast' to fit
the story from Scripture. When he came to the
words 'Belshazzar was slain', he instructed all

the instruments and voices to sound any note as loudly as possible in order to produce a huge, blaring discord on the word 'slain'. Belshazzar was finished.

God spoke to him through the hand writing on the wall to tell him that enough was enough. God would no longer watch while his people were mocked, his name was taken in vain and the sacred things were abused. God was stepping decisively back into history and bringing his judgement.

## Mercy and judgement

As we read the newspapers and watch the television news, we see over and over again how the world turns its back on God. Sometimes I look at our own country and wonder how long it can be before the hand of God metes out terrible punishments. And yet time goes on, and God is gracious, withholding his hand of judgement even though he could easily step in and say to our generation, 'Enough is enough.'

I believe that God is angry with the obscenities of our time, and I believe that we no longer say from our pulpits what should be said: that our corporate sin offends a holy God. I don't just mean a lapse in moral standards, the promiscuity that has, for example, produced AIDS and other diseases; that is only one of our sins. I think God is equally angry with a society that maltreats the poor and abuses the underprivileged; he is angry with a world in which people are set against each other by the colour of their skins; he is angry with any society where prejudice occurs, or where a caste system sets people in classes because of the accident of birth; he is angry at cultures where women are oppressed and downtrodden, where they die in childbirth because of lack of love and care in a male-dominated society. God is angry with a world that so abuses the gift of freedom that these sins are the result.

Sometimes God's judgement does come, and sometimes it is a judgement based on the sin. AIDS is a judgement – not on individual homosexuals, but on promiscuity as a whole. The disease is the natural fruit of the sinful behaviour – and, like many consequences of sin, its effects are felt by the innocent as well as the guilty.

But often God stays his hand, and continues to exercise restraint and mercy. We have the opportunity to look around and correct the sins of our society while there is still time. We have no guarantee of how long God will hold back, before saying, 'The writing is on the wall – you have been weighed on the scales and found wanting.'

## The failure of the church

A song by Graham Kendrick sums up all this. In it he writes, 'O Lord, the clouds are gathering' – and the clouds do indeed gather over any generation which turns its back on God.

O Lord, you stand appalled to see
Your laws of love so scorned
And lives so broken...
O Lord, over the nations now

Where is the dove of peace?
Her wings are broken.
O Lord, while precious children starve
The tools of war increase,
Their bread is stolen.
Have mercy, Lord.
Forgive us, Lord.

© Make Way Music/Thankyou Music 1987. PO Box 77, Hailsham, E. Sussex BN27 3EF.

One evening, not long ago, I came out from a
church meeting; a fight had broken out in the road
and an ambulance had been called. It was a grim
reminder of the truth we had just been singing
about in the same song: 'O Lord, dark powers are
poised to flood our streets with hate and fear.'
There was violence on our streets at the close of an
evening's celebration of the Christian truth. What
did it have to do with us?

It is not just the world that is in danger of judgement, but also the church. God has commanded us
to share the good news, to speak out for Christ.
Instead, what happens? We fail to take God seriously, and we shut ourselves in our churches away
from the rest of the world.

### Too little reverence

Belshazzar's final act of defiance was to treat the sacred things – the goblets set aside for worship in the
temple – as though they were ordinary.

You, O Belshazzar, have not humbled yourself...in-
stead, you have set yourself up against the Lord of
heaven. You had the goblets from his temple brought

to you...you praised the gods of silver...you did not honour the God who holds in his hand your life and all
your ways (Dan 5:22–23).

Within the church we treat the sacred things very
casually and carelessly. We study the Bible and we
think we know a lot about it; we keep going to
prayer meetings of one sort and another; we hum
hymn tunes and play Christian music while we're
doing the washing up – all very good things. Yet it is
so easy, through this very familiarity, to lose the
sense of the 'otherness' of God. Our church fellowship is so much part of our everyday life that we
become blasé about it, and treat the divine with a
casualness that is a sin.

For this we are in danger of being judged by God:
not in the sense of being rejected by him, but in the
sense of being distant from his will, so that our
prayers become ineffective and our worship hollow.
God is not impressed by any lifestyle – however full
of 'religious' activities – which does not see him as a
holy God. He longs not only to bring a sick world
back in line with him, but to recall to his will a casual,
flippant and half-hearted church.

We need prophets to speak out to the world and
say, 'You have not honoured God who has your life
in his hands. You have not honoured the God who
knows you.' And in the church we need prophets
who will say to us, 'You haven't really looked at the
God who has creation in his hands, who can send a
hand to write on the wall and warn of judgement;
you have not treated him with holy awe.'

*Too much pride*

There is a second sin which we share with Belshazzar: that of pride.

> O king, the Most High God gave your father Nebuchad-
> nezzar sovereignty and greatness and glory and splen-
> dour...But when his heart became arrogant and har-
> dened with pride, he was deposed from his royal throne
> ...But you his son, O Belshazzar, have not humbled your-
> self, though you knew all this (Dan 5:18, 20, 22).

Pride can be a very subtle sin. After my first book
was published, several people said to me, 'Now
you're getting your picture in all these magazines,
you won't get arrogant about it, will you?' And of
course I didn't – in fact, I'm proud to say how humble I am! You win twice that way – you can be proud
and people think you're humble.

Pride is a problem for all of us, whether or not we're
in the public eye. Pride is the desire to be acclaimed, to
be noticed, to do things our way or to have what we
want; we may take pride in our achievements, our
accomplishments, even our attitudes.

One of Satan's greatest tricks is to make us proud
in the spiritual gifts given by God. God blesses us
and fills us with his Spirit, he gives us his gifts – and
then we let Satan spoil that by making us proud that
we have something other people don't have. If only
the whole church was as faithful, as free, as filled as
we are, we say. And at once we're pointing the finger
at other people, puffing ourselves up with pride.
The church as a whole may pride itself on its
evangelism, or its young people's programmes, or its

staff, or its size – how sad that a sign of God's blessing can be turned into an excuse for arrogance.

As soon as we take our eyes off God and fix them on gifts, or leadership, or authority, we are treating God casually, taking pride in ourselves, and becoming judgemental and critical of other people. It's not an attractive picture. In fact, in some churches, the main thing which stops Christians coming into the fullness of the Spirit is the spectacle of the kind of people who do claim to be Spirit-filled. Their arrogance about what God has done does not draw people in, but rather repels them.

Of course, sometimes there is pride on the other side, too. 'The church got on fine for centuries without all these spiritual gifts,' people object. In actual fact, historical evidence shows that that's probably not true, but what arrogance to say, 'No, thank you, God, I don't want those gifts.' How can we possibly dare to choose, or refuse, what God wants to give us? Again, it is a rejection of the holiness and power and wisdom of God, and the setting up of ourselves and our will in pride. We are sharing in Belshazzar's sins and we risk sharing in his downfall.

## The voice of honesty

We need to confess our pride and take God's holiness seriously. Only then can we fulfil the true work of the church in the world: proclaiming the good news and telling people what God is really like.

### Daniel

If Belshazzar is an example of the consequences of

pride and ignoring God, Daniel shows us what our response to God should be like. He was called to be set apart, to be God's man, and he resisted any temptation to pride, any temptation to compromise God's message, any temptation to sell out to the powerful people who ran his society.

Belshazzar said to Daniel,

> I have heard that you are able to give interpretations and to solve difficult problems. If you can read this writing and tell me what it means, you will be clothed in purple and have a gold chain laced round your neck, and you will be made the third highest ruler in the kingdom (Dan 5:16).

Daniel was offered rich clothing (wearing purple in the ancient world was the prerogative of kings and nobles), signs of honour in the gold chain, and power – money, social standing, and the approval of the king. Who could refuse?

Daniel could. He answered, 'You may keep your gifts for yourself and give your rewards to someone else. Nevertheless, I will read the writing for the king and tell him what it means' (Dan 5:17). What a refreshing character!

We shouldn't forget that Daniel wasn't about to tell Belshazzar what a good king he was. It doesn't cross Daniel's mind to take the money and run, because he would need protection once the king got to hear that his days were numbered and his worst enemies were going to become king.

This story is an exciting one because it's a prelude to the more familiar story of Daniel in the lions' den.

The reason why Daniel could stand unflinching in the den of lions was that he'd had practice standing before Belshazzar. His character had already been tested. He could have said he'd forgotten how to do interpretations. Or he could have said he didn't fancy interpreting this particular vision. Or he could have interpreted it but toned it down a little: 'Your days are numbered but there are still quite a few left; you've been weighed and you're just a little on the light side, maybe you could work at that a bit?' Instead he went straight to the heart of the matter and told the truth – God's truth – faithfully and without compromise, in spite of the possible consequences for himself.

*Standing firm*

I believe that there is a message here for the church of Jesus. We live in a society where sin is rife, pride is commonplace and where people treat God with disdain. We are called to speak out with uncompromising honesty, like Daniel. We are called to speak out on television, in the press, in politics, in our communities, to bring the message of God to our world today.

But we are easily bought off, because it's painful to be critical of society in public. If the church speaks out it will be cut off from positions of power, ignored or ridiculed by the press, marginalised by politicians. It is a costly thing to be an uncompromising agent of God in this world, but Daniel shows us that it can be done.

It isn't only the world which tries to put pressure on us to conform: other Christians often do so, too.

Whenever we become really fired with an awareness of God's will, someone is always ready to call us a fanatic. Even in the most Spirit-filled churches, anyone equipped by God for an unpopular or unexpected task will be suspected of too much zeal. But it's better to err on the side of enthusiasm – God finds it easier to cool down a fanatic than to warm up a corpse!

Within any congregation there are pressure groups urging more emphasis on this or that, or less frequent mention of the other. We need to recall the words of the old hymn:

> Riches I heed not, nor man's empty praise,
> Be thou mine inheritance now and always.
> Be thou and thou only the first in my heart,
> O Sovereign of heaven, my treasure thou art.

We must be known as Christians, not because of our pride or arrogance or prickliness or disapproval, but because we reflect the love of God, and because we've been baptised with his fire which sets us apart. The factory, the office, the school, the supermarket can all be lions' dens where it's hard to be a Christian, to walk in a holy way and stand up for what we believe. But God can touch us with his power and give us the grace he gave Daniel, to stand firm for God and bear witness to his love, his power and his holiness.

# 10

## *The Nature of the Kingdom*

In the last few chapters we have looked, in turn, at God's forgiveness, his love and his holiness, and the call to the church to acceptance, to love, and to honesty. These images begin to give us more idea of the nature of the kingdom of God.

### The authority of the kingdom

The United Kingdom is a geographical area – we can define its borders and the position of its land masses. The kingdom of God is different. The word used in the New Testament comes from an Aramaic word meaning rulership or kingship, or the area over which a certain person's authority extends. In other words, if a slave was sent by his owner on a mission to another city or country, he would still be under his owner's jurisdiction, wherever he was. The authority was not geographical, but personal. The slave owed allegiance to his master whether he was in Jerusalem, Antioch or Rome.

Similarly, we are Christians within the kingdom of God, whether we live in England or America or Africa. Our allegiance is first to the kingdom of God, and only secondly to the country where we find ourselves living.

This idea was revolutionary dynamite in the first century AD when inhabitants of the Roman Empire were expected to promise allegiance to Rome. Christians who proclaimed, 'Jesus is Lord,' would not also say, 'Caesar is Lord,' and so they were constantly thought of as insurrectionists and rebels. They claimed to be members of a distinct kingdom, the kingdom of God – this kingdom is in the human heart where Jesus rules.

When Jesus began his ministry, he proclaimed, 'The kingdom is among you' – the kingdom was personified in Jesus, who cast out demons, healed the sick, raised the dead and preached the good news. He was the kingdom on earth – not the totality of the kingdom which is to come, but the ingrafting of God's kingdom into the lives of men and women there in the first century. What made this kingdom potent for all mankind was the death and resurrection of Jesus; by that door we enter into his kingdom and share in the benefits of eternal life.

We are sharing in that kingdom now, but there is a sense in which its fullness is still to come. We are awaiting the parousia, the time when Jesus comes again and for the second time steps into the history of this world. When that happens he will come in glory to be established as the Lord of every person's life, whether or not they want to bow the knee to him as Saviour.

## Kingdoms in conflict

However much we may long for that second coming and for the world to be restored to its original perfection, it is important to realise that God's kingdom has in fact already arrived. It is true that we suffer from the activities of Satan and from the sin and pain he causes; it is true that we are in a state of conflict. But it is not the case that God is on one side, Satan on the other, and we hope the right side wins. Rather, the victory has already been won.

When the Second World War ended, the German and Japanese leaders signed surrender documents and the war was officially over. The Allied forces had won. Yet for years after 1945 there were sporadic outbursts of fighting, particularly in some of the more remote Japanese islands where groups of soldiers had not realised that the war was over. They continued in the conflict, even though the Allied 'kingdom' had been established.

In a similar way, God's kingdom has been established by the death and resurrection of Jesus: Satan has been defeated. This period of history, from the ascension of Jesus to the second coming, is simply a time of mopping up the few remaining satanic troups who don't realise that it is all over. They continue to raise their rebel heads against God's kingdom, but there is no chance of their winning, because God's victory is already assured.

### *An awareness of mystery*

We don't always understand the implications of this continuing conflict, so there is a certain element of mystery in our Christian lives. Why do bad things happen to us? Why are our prayers not always answered? The answer is that we are still living in a period of conflict, so we can't expect everything now to be as one day it will be, when every sickness will be healed, every tear wiped away, and every circumstance sorted out in God's will.

For instance, why are the sick not always healed when we pray for them? Some people advance the theory that the sufferer simply does not have enough faith (not very comforting for them) as they try desperately to work up sufficient faith for the miracle to happen. Others suggest that the difficulty is that there is sin in their life – as if the rest of us didn't have that problem! The key to the answer lies in the fact that we are still in kingdom conflict. There are some prayers which are answered in a powerful way, as the future comes into the present and men and women are healed mentally, physically and spiritually. There are other occasions when this does not happen; it's no good pretending that we know why, or looking for someone to blame – either the sufferer or the person who prays – it's simply a mystery to us at the moment.

### A promise of victory

Yet we know that one day all these things will be revealed, because the future, in all its glorious perfection, is assured. We should have a sense of victory even amid the mystery and confusion of day-to-day living. Sometimes Christians miss out on the fact that we are actually on the winning side: we are part of the victory, not because we are good, but because

God is good. There is no doubt about the outcome of our personal salvation, weak and sinful though we are, because God's kingdom has already won, and its establishment is being worked out.

Another good example of this process is the abolition of slavery. When William Wilberforce and others managed to get the Act passed in 1833, that did not mean that every slave was freed on that day. It took a while to be worked out in practice, so that the slave owners could hear about it, the authorities could enforce it, and so that freed slaves could find homes and employment. Even after all this had been achieved in England, there were still distant parts of the British Empire where there were still slaves, because the law had not come fully into effect.

## Revolutionary relationships

The values of the kingdom are based around the issues of relationships. Luke 6 reveals a revolution in this area.

> But I tell you who hear me: Love your enemies, and do good to those who hate you, bless those who curse you, pray for those who ill-treat you. If someone strikes you on one cheek, turn to him the other also. If someone takes your cloak, do not stop him from taking your tunic. Give to everyone who asks you, and if anyone takes what belongs to you, do not demand it back. Do to others as you would have them do to you (Lk 6:27–31).

These were hardly the standards of the first-century world, and neither are they the standards of the world today. 'If someone strikes you on one cheek, hit him in the stomach, and if anyone takes what belongs to you, get it back fast, with a bit more if possible.' That's more like the behaviour of the ordinary world.

But we have another king, and we belong to a different kingdom; we live by his values. His kingdom extends as we demonstrate his values to others. If we just bleat on about the joys of Christianity but we don't live by Christ's standards, we are hypocrites and the world sees right through us.

Living by Christ's standards is not easy. If we have been mistreated by someone we pray for them, but our prayers may be subtly vindictive: 'Lord, I pray that you will bring them to repentance.' Our minds race ahead: 'And if that can be a painful process, so much the better.' We may not say it out loud, but we secretly hope that pain will come to others because they have brought pain to us. Sometimes we wrap it all up in super-spirituality and say that when bad things do happen to people, it's because God is judging them. But in fact that is our carnality which has surfaced, betraying the kingdom values of loving, blessing and praying, no matter what comes our way.

Part of the trouble is something we looked at earlier in the book – our insistence on our rights. We have a right to be angry when someone is unkind to us. We have a right to reclaim our own when things are taken from us. But the kingdom calls us not to our rights but to our privileges, given by the King himself. We are privileged to exercise his role in the world by demonstrating his values: turning the other cheek demonstrates our commitment to the

Servant King, who is the victor.

*At home*

Every time we bring another area of our life under God's kingly rule, his kingdom is extended. The close personal relationships we have in the home should be the first to come under scrutiny. It's too easy just to go through the motions of married life, without exercising these values there. Some marriages are marriages in name only, the home merely a building where two strangers live separate lives, resenting any encroachment on their time.

We need to understand what kingdom values mean in terms of sexuality, too. We have to push away the worldly values which say that sex outside marriage is acceptable, with a partner of the same sex, or with any number of partners. It will need an army of young people prepared to be virgins until the day they marry to push back the tide of worldly values.

We must practise marital fidelity, too, so that we can be certain that our relationship is one in which Christ is honoured and glorified. In the film *Fatal Attraction* a man has an affair with a woman over one weekend, and as a result his whole life becomes distorted and ultimately is destroyed, until right at the end he and his wife manage to salvage the dying remains of a broken marriage. I wish everyone contemplating an affair could see that film, to understand what infidelity means in terms of human sadness and pain.

The motto of the world in these areas is 'freedom', and the myth is that promiscuity makes us happy

because we can do what we want. The opposite is
true: it does not bring peace or freedom but anguish
and destruction – to family life, children and
parents, friends and relations. Too often, now, it
carries with it the risk of AIDS and other diseases.

The answer to AIDS, frankly, is not condoms but
chastity. We should not arrogantly declare, 'We've
got it right and you've got it wrong,' but back up the
truth of what we say with gentle, humble lives.

It's not just sexual relationships that are subject to
these standards. How many of us as husbands have a
pastoral concern and a kind word for everyone in
the church, but at home are like a bear with a sore
head? How many wives are sensitive, sweet and
reasonable until the family drawbridge is pulled up;
then they become nagging and critical? That is not
kingdom living. Kingdom values are not about
vague theological issues, they are about real people
in real situations, living out what Jesus says about
family life.

*At work*

If people see the kingdom values lived out in our
lives they will want more and more of what we have.
At work these values may be expressed in our integrity, because honesty is one of the standards set by
the kingdom. We must live by what the Bible
teaches, openly and bravely, even when by our
actions we condemn the usual practices of our workmates. Whenever we slip from those high standards,
we are letting our workplace come under the rule of
the Prince of darkness, whether it is in gossip and
backbiting, casual attitudes to expense claims, or

simple slacking about doing a fair day's work.

Of course, we don't have total control over what goes on in our place of work, and sometimes it may be very difficult for the light of Jesus to shine there. Our superiors may make life harder for us, there may be tensions with workmates or with those for whom we have responsibility. Yet we can always try, to the best of our ability, to live out God's values by what we say and do. Through prayer, through words and example, the workplace can be progressively won back for the kingdom of God.

### In the community

How is the community to know that there is an exciting new kingdom beyond the bounds of the familiar? Only by seeing us as we demonstrate the kingdom values in our relationships. We are the ambassadors for that kingdom, the representatives of God in the world.

Often when there is serious trouble in a country – war or civil unrest – other countries begin to withdraw their embassy staff. The diplomats, clerical staff and ambassadors return to the safety of their home countries until the situation settles down. But we don't have that luxury: we can't withdraw from the kingdom of Satan and return when it seems convenient. We are permanent, resident ambassadors wherever God has placed us to represent his kingly rule.

Some of us get good locations where people are well-disposed towards our message; others are ambassadors in more difficult places, but God will bless our work wherever we are.

*In the church*

It ought to be easier to live out the values of the kingdom in the church – after all, we're all on the same side, working towards the same goal. Maybe we still slip into our carnal ways occasionally, but we forgive each other and build one another up in love – don't we?

The standards and values for kingdom living are found in the Bible. This can be a great release for those of us who have perhaps grown up thinking that we were involved not so much in the kingdom of God as in the kingdom of the church. Too often we have been locked into all sorts of attitudes and behaviour patterns which we have come to believe are kingdom standards, when really they are just church standards. For example, morning worship happens at ten thirty or it isn't the real thing; communion happens at the end of a service, not the beginning.

I remember when I was a youngster going to church in a coloured shirt for the first time. I noticed a few strange looks during the service, and not a little disapproval. I went home and started looking in the Bible for the verse that told us about it – and of course it was very difficult to find anything about white shirts, or grey or blue or red ones, apart from the multicoloured coat worn by Joseph.

I was a lot older before I understood what had really been going on that day: the exalting of church values to something much more important. It doesn't matter a scrap to God whether we meet at six thirty or ten thirty or three in the morning, wearing pyjamas – in fact there are good reasons why we don't meet at three am, but they are not anything to do with the Bible, or the values that really matter in the church.

Values of tradition and culture may be helpful or they may be stifling. We may ignore them if we choose, or we may obey them so as not to give offence; but it is our choice. The real question is what are God's values; what does Scripture say and how are we to interpret it, how are we to live out the life of the kingdom in our church? These are the things which set us free and make us the servants of the King.

## A relationship with the King

All the revolutionary relationships described in Luke 6 – loving, blessing, returning good for evil – are to be worked out in all places and situations – home, work, community, church. But they depend on one prior relationship: our relationship with God.

For example, I am a husband and a father, but the priority relationship is the husband. The best thing I can do for my children is to love their mother, so that being a husband is what enables the second relationship – being a father – to function.

In God's kingdom I am God's son first, and because I have that role, I am in a position to minister to other people. All relationships with others flow from the fact that we are in a relationship with God; if that is not so, then all these other relationships are just empty words. As 1 Corinthians 4:20 says, 'The kingdom of God is not a matter of talk but of power' – it's a matter of action.

This situation is the opposite of the political situation in Great Britain, where the Queen as monarch has no genuine authority. She is the Head of State, and the Prime Minister takes the various Bills passed through Parliament for the Queen to sign. If the Queen were ever to say, 'I won't sign that,' a constitutional crisis would be provoked, and I doubt whether the Prime Minister would lose. But if that were to happen the whole political structure of the country would be altered.

We often treat God as though he were this sort of monarch: 'Lord, I've got this and that lined up for the next few years, please bless this plan and that one, and after that I'm not sure what to do, so if you've got any ideas I'd quite like to hear them.' We run our lives ourselves, and ask God to rubber-stamp our plans with his approval and blessing. Of course, when we really need something we rush off to him with our requests – some healing, please, a bit more money, maybe a little more success – but mainly we just want the rubber stamp.

In fact God's values have been written down for us to follow, and he wants to guide us all the time by his Spirit so that we can walk in his way and do his will. In God's kingdom he is King. Everything we do should be guided by God: we should be saying, 'Lord, what do you want done here? In this situation, with my family or friends, what values do you want me to demonstrate? In my home, my work, community life, the church, what is it that you want done?' Some people find it very helpful to pray, 'Jesus, you walked on earth as the kingdom personified. If you were faced with this problem, what would you do?' The kingdom values come through us as we invite Jesus to exercise his authority in what we do.

This is a tremendous opportunity, a great challenge and privilege. We are the servants of the true King, of the ultimate authority, who wants to establish his kingdom more and more in our world, our country, our street. Wherever we are, we are like the rays of sunlight at the dawn of a new day, as the sun comes up and the darkness is pushed back. The light is creeping across our land, shining in more and more hearts, until the time when the King comes in glory to claim his own and the kingdom is established in all its fullness.

# 11

## Resources for the Kingdom

What does God need to establish his kingdom? What can he use to bring about his will for this world which he loved so much that he gave his life for it?

First, he needs people. The kingdom will not be won by a computer, and we will never teach a machine to pray for the sick. God needs ordinary men and women, whether volunteering for full-time missionary work, or just ready to serve him in their everyday lives at home, school and in the workplace.

Secondly, those people need to be equipped. It's no good having a willing volunteer saying, 'Lord, I'm here,' if that person is not ready to be equipped spiritually and given the tools for the job.

There used to be a TV advert for government training, where a huge rectangular block of stone was chiselled away until it became a cylinder. Then it was lowered by crane into a cylindrical hole into which it fitted perfectly. The implication was that 'you can't put a square peg in a round hole' – that there are lots of jobs available, but that people need to be trained to do them.

My own father has recently taken early retirement, and he is now involved in retraining on one day a week. He used to be a teacher, but he now thinks he'd like to go into something less stressful. He knows that he needs new skills and new ideas to come into the labour market, but he's willing to spend some time learning them.

In the same way, if we want to do the work which God has planned for us, we should be willing to allow the Holy Spirit to equip us.

## Untapped potential

The church often fails to utilise people's potential. It fails to tap into the vast resources represented by those people who are seldom offered the chance to use their skills and abilities because of prejudice and tradition.

### The young

Churches often have a fairly patronising attitude to young people. Many churches have a diaconate, or a group of elders, or a church council in which it is difficult to find anyone who is not retired. It's true that the church needs age, wisdom and experience; but we also need enthusiasm and fresh ideas, and if we refuse to use the resources of young people which God has provided, we will fail to be a church which is relevant for today. Young people are not the church of tomorrow, they are the church of today, and we need them to challenge our presuppositions, and their exuberance to temper our caution. The church needs both authority and power, wisdom and energy, and we need to balance our use of those resources.

In some countries of the world, growth is so rapid that half the population is under sixteen. British Youth for Christ says that there are one billion young people who need to know the Lord. To reach young people, we need young people – not alone, but strengthened by the wisdom and support of the rest of the church. What we must not do is to trivialise the contribution of the young to our church life.

Paul said to Timothy, 'Let no man despise you because of your youth.' David Pawson once spoke about the death of Samson, when he destroyed the temple of Dagon and thousands of Philistines and their leaders. He pointed out that when Samson, blind and weak, came out to perform his last feat of strength he was led by a young man, a servant, who placed his hands on the pillars which supported the pagan temple. He suggested that the young people of today can be like that young man, leading a fragmented, weakened church to a place of power once more.

I would never wish to minimise the role of experience and maturity, and neither do I wish to see new young converts pushed too quickly into leadership. The characteristic most needed in any Christian is the humility to be a willing servant of God, in whatever role we are given: arrogance robs us of the opportunity to be useful. Yet too often we ignore the gifts of the young, simply because of their age, and that is a prejudice of which we should be ashamed.

## Women

Here we move into a slightly more controversial area. I believe that in women the church has a resource for ministry and leadership which it has tended to ignore for years. Frankly, I feel that the way many churches have treated women in their congregations is nothing less than sinful.

Over and over again, women have been marginalised and excluded from positions of authority in the church. Indeed, the church has had the arrogance to send women out onto the missionfield alone, to preach the gospel in horrendous situations which have frightened off many men; and then in the home church they are relegated to the tea committee. That is not what the Bible teaches about the role of women in the church.

In the Bible we meet women like Deborah, the great judge who led the people of Israel to do marvellous things; Esther who had such an impact on the ancient world; the Marys and Martha and the other women who were in the entourage of Jesus, ministering to him and caring for him.

## The 'fishermen'

People often criticise the church for being too middle class, or only for intellectuals. Have you ever noticed how often we appoint to positions of leadership professional people who have a degree? It's very easy for the church to become qualification-conscious and academically oriented. Of course we should use these people who have a great deal to offer, but we need a wider understanding of leadership.

Look at Jesus' disciples. We can't get away from the fact that even among the first twelve they had an accountant! So I'm quite happy to have that profession represented in our church leadership team. But James and John, Peter and Andrew were all fishermen, people who worked with their hands, like the people among whom Jesus lived for most of his life. We must be careful not to place barriers around leadership; we must not make paper qualifications a reason for being a leader, nor an articulate manner nor a good business record. Someone with a limited formal education may have a heart that is centred on God, and sense something of him that the more 'intellectual' person may never have seen.

God wants to raise up a church that is not class-conscious. We should be sharing leadership and working in ministry together because we love the Lord, not because we have a label – working class, upper class, educated, uneducated, or whatever. The crucial questions are whether we are walking faithfully with the Lord, and whether we have integrity in our ministry.

## Singles

In the family of the church it's easy to become family-centred, preferring leaders to be married and youth workers to be parents. However, there are more single people than ever before in our communities. This is partly because people tend to get married later nowadays, but there are other reasons: an increase in divorce, and the fact that men generally die earlier than women, so that many women are widowed in middle or later life. If we limit leadership to married people because of blind prejudice, we rob ourselves of vast resources of manpower, energy and enthusiasm.

Too many people are either ignorant of the needs of single people or else they are patronising. They may invite someone for lunch in a tone that suggests that it's a favour: 'It must be really tough being single, and we'd like to have you at our house because we're good-hearted people.' There is an unspoken suggestion that people are not whole if they are not married, but that is simply not true in God's scheme of things. He is interested in individuals, as well as couples; every life has value and purpose in itself.

## Spiritual resources

God has provided the people in our churches, but it's up to us to use them to the full. But people need spiritual resources to do God's will, and that means being constantly open to the prompting of the Holy Spirit, to accept and use the gifts he wants to give us.

### Gifts

> There are different kinds of gifts, but the same Spirit. There are different kinds of service, but the same Lord. There are different kinds of working, but the same God works in all of them in all men (1 Cor 12:4–6).

The tools for God's work are gifts and ministries –

the Bible makes a distinction, but as far as we are concerned they have this in common: they are given by God for our use.

Sometimes we become so obsessed by spiritual gifts that we forget that they are supposed to be used, not admired. If someone prays in tongues or brings a prophetic word in church, there's often a great deal of talk about it afterwards: 'Wasn't that great? God was with us in that service.' But if you ask, 'Well, what did God say?' people can't remember; they have become obsessed with the gift itself and not with its purpose.

Spiritual gifts are not given for inside the church, but outside; not for Sunday services but for Monday to Saturday living. Gifts and ministries are the tools for the job.

One day, shortly before I was married, I was driving my fiancée to the airport in my rather battered old car. Suddenly we had a puncture and I realised, with a sinking heart, that I was going to have to change the wheel. I jacked the car up all right, but I couldn't get the wheel nuts off; I had the proper spanner but no matter how hard I pushed and pulled, I couldn't loosen them. In the end we had to call the RAC. I felt really foolish that I wasn't strong enough to do the job.

The breakdown van arrived, and out climbed a huge mechanic, about seven feet tall, with a spanner that looked twice the size of mine. He put it on one of the nuts, pulled it and pushed it with his foot, but he couldn't shift it either. I felt wonderful – I wasn't a weakling after all! Then he went back to his van and came back with a long metal pipe which he fixed to the spanner. He went to the end of it and leaned on it, and with all that leverage the thing shifted at last. So he changed the wheel for us and off we went.

Now, the moral of all this is that I could easily have become obsessed with spanner-sizes and pieces of pipe, vowing that I would never travel anywhere without a piece of pipe exactly like the one produced by the breakdown service. However, the pipe alone couldn't carry us and the luggage to Gatwick: it had a specific job to do. In the same way, the importance of gifts and ministries lies in what they can accomplish, not in themselves.

## Unity

> The body is a unit, though it is made up of many parts; and though all its parts are many, they form one body...There should be no division in the body, but...its parts should have equal concern for each other (1 Cor 12:12,25).

Spiritual gifts gain their true power when we function together. If we turn spiritual gifts into an ego trip, checking out who has more gifts than anyone else, we get nowhere because we are not working in harmony. We need to operate together in exercising the gifts and ministries of the Holy Spirit, whether it is in the housegroup, the prayer group, the home, or the gathering for corporate worship. We are the people of God, and we need each other.

## Humility

'Those parts of the body that seem to be weaker are

indispensable, and the parts we think are less honourable we treat with special honour' (1 Cor 12:22-23). If we exercise these gifts with humility, we should not believe that our gifts are more important than anyone else's.

George Whitefield and John Wesley were great preachers in their day, but their followers were rivals. One supporter asked George Whitefield, 'Do you think we will see John Wesley in heaven?'

'No,' Whitefield replied.

The disciple was thrilled with this fuel for criticism, so he went on, 'Why?'

'We won't see John Wesley in heaven,' answered Whitefield, 'because he will be too near the throne.'

That great man understood about another's ministry – he didn't try to tear it down, but build it up.

There is no point in examining gifts for superiority or importance; in thinking that having the gift of tongues is better than having the gift of hospitality. The Bible says that all the gifts are to be honoured and valued, and we need humility to do that.

### Desire

'But eagerly desire the greater gifts' (1 Cor 12:31). Acting with humility does not mean that we sit back to see whether God feels like giving us a gift: we know he wants to equip us for his purposes. To say that we don't need equipping is merely adolescent spirituality. The hallmark of adolescence is the claim, 'I can do it.' When I was fourteen I knew a lot about the world and I realised that my dad didn't know much. By the time I got to twenty-one my dad had learned quite a bit!

I preached my first sermon at the age of fourteen in a small village church in Lancashire. The following Sunday I preached at an after-church meeting in Southport. Sixteen people attended and four of them became Christians that night. 'Well, what's the point of college?' I thought. 'What do I need training for? I bet the Lord is thinking he's glad he's got Steve Gaukroger on his side. Maybe I could do a term or so at college and then start lecturing!' My terrible, overbearing confidence was a sign of my adolescent spirituality.

In fact, we all need to be empowered by the Holy Spirit to be the men and women God wants us to be. We need his guidance and his gifts, and we must long for those things because that is how God will use us.

### Godliness

The sum total of all these spiritual resources is godliness. As we desire the spiritual resources which will enable us to work for God's kingdom, as we exercise them in unity and humility, our one aim is to be the people of God, doing his will. That is godly living.

No matter who you are, single or married, educated or uneducated, man or woman, young or old, the goal of godliness will bring you to a position of valuable ministry. Never ridicule the tools which the supernatural kingdom needs; be open to all the gifts God wants to give you. 'Blessed are those who hunger and thirst for righteousness, for they will be filled' (Mt 5:6).

All that the kingdom needs for its establishment in this world is people – God's people – willing to strive for godliness, and open to receive all that the Spirit longs to give us.

# 12

## *Ordering Your Private World*

We all long for peace, for a calm outlook on life, for a quiet spirit. How do we arrive at this? 'You will keep in perfect peace him whose mind is steadfast because he trusts in you' (Is 26:3). The word 'mind' in the Bible does not just refer to the part of us which does the thinking, but to the deeper part of our being, our true selves. What Isaiah is saying is that peace is the result not of living a life without problems, nor the absence of stress or tension, but of having a mind stayed on God, trusting him and centred on him in all we do.

In the New Testament we find Jesus speaking to the Pharisees:

Make a tree good and its fruit will be good, or make a tree bad and its fruit will be bad, for a tree will be recognised by its fruit. You brood of vipers, how can you who are evil say anything good? For out of the overflow of the heart the mouth speaks. The good man brings good

things out of the good stored up in him, and the evil
man brings evil things out of the evil stored up in him
(Mt 12:33–35).

The Pharisees, of course, were great ones for the
external observances of law and ritual, but Jesus fre-
quently accused them of being empty: they kept up
the appearance of devotion, but there was no true
devotion in their hearts. The crucial phrase occurs
in verse 34: 'Out of the overflow of the heart the
mouth speaks.' It is a biblical principle that we can
keep up appearances for all we're worth, but our
speech, our habits, our attitudes all betray us, They
spring from the heart, showing who we *really* are,
not the people the rest of the church thinks we are,
or the people we would like to be.

This is why it can be a waste of time to organise
programmes aimed at improving people's Christianity. Calling people to godly living is like rearranging
the deckchairs on the Titanic: no matter how tidy
you get them, the ship is still going to sink. You can
teach people to evangelise, or work harder at
prayer, or improve the worship, or whatever, but
unless the inner being is right with God, all that
effort is futile. What matters is the private world, the
world no one sees except God: if that is not 'steadfast' and trusting in God, all our external devotion is
empty.

*Deceptive appearances*

In any church there are people who seem to have
their act together. Their lifestyle seems sensible, and
their spiritual life mature. There is no way other

people can see what they are disguising, what is lurking inside them, what they are always afraid they will give away by a careless word: that their hearts are not right with God.

Recently I was travelling with the family, and we stopped at a service station which shall be nameless. We collected our tea from the self-service counter and I went off to make a phone call. While I was gone, Bethany wandered over to the stack of empty trays and called, 'Mummy, there's something down here!' My wife went over to see, and there behind the tray stack was a mouse!

Now the service station looked spotless, and it was full of people eating their meals in perfect confidence and with great enjoyment. We would have been doing the same, if my daughter hadn't been so curious. But after that, it was very difficult to relax and eat anything: the appearance of the place was deceptive.

I'm not suggesting that we should be inquisitorial about our fellow Christians – far from it – rather, we need to look closely at ourselves. We can fool ourselves with our deceptive appearances, just as the Pharisees did. Yet there may be small things hidden in the depth of our being which are gnawing away at us, keeping our hearts from the standards of purity and steadfastness which God requires.

It can be a terrifying experience when we suddenly come face to face with our real selves. Sometimes we have an unexpected flash of self-revelation: waking in the middle of the night, or walking along the road in a moment of silence, in a crisis, or in the calm of an idle moment. All at once the din of everyday activity ceases to drown out the reality of who we really are. Is that true self given wholly to God?

## Under new management

What happens when we first see our true selves? For most of us, it's part of a process which has been bringing us closer to God. It's rather like an old building which is run down and poorly looked after by its owners; when new owners take over they put up a big sign saying, 'Under New Management'. Our lives are going downhill until Jesus takes over. No matter how many coats of paint we put on the outside, the woodworm and dry rot are there underneath. When Jesus comes into our lives we are under new management, but we aren't totally renewed at that moment – there's a lot of work to be done.

The new manager of the run-down building has to go from room to room to redecorate, shore up and cut out the diseased wood and fit it out so that people can work or live in the place. In the same way, our hearts still contain the clutter of failure and error and pain from the past, the cracks caused by Satan, and the wallpaper we've pasted over to hide them. We need to come to Jesus for continuing healing and wholeness, but we must first be aware of where precisely we need Jesus to help and heal us.

Many of us have believed for too long that Christianity is just a series of actions. We must read the Bible and pray every day; we must go to church regularly; we must do this and that in order to be a good Christian. Most of these things are good in themselves, but they are externals. They are like the speech which springs from the heart: unless the heart is right, the externals will never come right, and our reading will never flower into wisdom, and our churchgoing will never flower into worship.

What is really necessary is a change of heart: we need to change so that our heart is centred on God, so that our private world is one where Jesus is Lord.

## Why should we change?

Why do we need to reorder our private world? Why is it important that we should become the sort of Christians whose hearts are set on God alone? There are four main reasons.

### For God's sake

God longs that every person in the world should experience the new birth and come into the kingdom so that they may have life 'and have it to the full' (Jn 10:10) free of all the pains and secret miseries that drag us down. When we focus our innermost being on the living God these things are made possible, and that brings God joy.

We know what pleases our wife or husband or friends because we know them. What pleases God is an undivided heart, a being that is totally focused on him as far as is possible at our particular stage of spiritual development. As we move closer to God, our ability to trust him increases; we are able to open our hearts to him and make him Lord of our whole life.

There are usually parts of our lives that we don't look into too closely ourselves; we certainly keep them hidden from our friends, and we would really rather God didn't see them either. There are sins we don't want to give up because we enjoy them, attitudes we spiritualise to make them seem acceptable, and actions we excuse because we don't want to deal with them. But if we want to bring God joy, we have to let him shine into those dark, hidden places and show up all the things we haven't confessed because we don't want to throw them out.

The problem with this reluctance to clear out the dustier corners of our hearts is that it affects the rest of our lives. You know how it's possible to have a conversation and think of something else at the same time – only half-listening – until someone says accusingly, 'You haven't heard a word I've been saying!' If we are worried about something or afraid of something, it occupies our mind so that our thoughts keep coming back to it, no matter what else we do. In the same way on the spiritual level our words, actions and attitudes always wander back to the priorities which fill our hearts: 'out of the overflow of the heart the mouth speaks'.

Jesus said, 'Where your treasure is, there your heart will be also' (Lk 12:34). If we value material things, they are our treasure, and that's what our hearts will be preoccupied with; if we enjoy malice or gossip, that will fill our hearts; but if we value God, he is our treasure and our hearts are his. It gives God joy to draw us closer to him, heal our pain and give us life 'to the full'.

*For our sake*

Secondly, we need to order our private world for

our own sake. When there are gnawing, unforgiven sins, emotional hurts which have not been healed, works of Satan not yet rooted out, we live in pain. That pain affects the way we live and the way we respond to other people.

We sing about it in the hymn:

What a friend we have in Jesus,
All our sins and grief to bear!
What a privilege to carry
Everything to God in prayer!
Oh, what peace we often forfeit,
Oh, what needless pain we bear
All because we do not carry
Everything to God in prayer!

We forfeit peace because the inner life in turmoil reverberates through our emotions into the rest of our life – 'out of the overflow of the heart' – and we bear unnecessary pain because Jesus is waiting to heal us of every hurt. We live in tension and insecurity and lack of peace because our inner life is not focused on God. So for our own sake we should reorder our private world.

### For the sake of the body

Another result of this inner turmoil is that we lose our vision for the church. When we are merely acting out a lifestyle, while our hearts are not really committed to it, we end up with a kind of spiritual double vision. We view everything through our own pain and confusion, and fail to see the true picture.

I often meet people with criticisms or rigid attitudes about what is going on in the church, and it soon becomes clear that they are not speaking out of a sense of oneness with God, but out of a view which is terribly marred by an inner duplicity of spirit. (There are lots of other people who criticise the church constructively and in a loving spirit!) If you are operating on a spiritual double standard, your view of spiritual reality is bound to be distorted.

Similarly, if we come to worship with a divided heart, our prayers and praises and singing will all be half-hearted, and the whole church loses out. We owe it to the rest of the body of Christ to build up our fellowship, not tear it down!

*For the sake of the world*

In my experience, when the Christian's heart is not centred on God, the first thing to suffer is evangelism. If you yourself are insecure, unsure of the vitality and importance of your faith, you are in no state to reach out to others. So for the sake of the world which is waiting to hear the good news of Jesus' love from our lips, we need to change our lives and centre them on God.

## How can we change?

So how do we go about reordering our private world, making God the centre of our lives? In one sense it is a process which takes a lifetime, as we continually turn to him and ask him to fill our hearts. There is no easy formula for this profound change of direction, this deep inner healing. But there are some key steps to receiving God's touch.

## Recognising the need

There is no need for us to start grubbing around in our hearts looking for bad things: that merely leads to a kind of spiritual neurosis. But it is true that there are parts of our minds and hearts where God's Spirit is needing to work; areas which we prefer not to examine.

We talk about our Christian joy, for instance, when often what we really mean is that happy feeling we get from a fine sunny day. True Christian joy is that powerful trust in God which can overcome all adversity and suffering, but we only find it when God has done a deep work in our lives.

So the first step is to recognise that we need God's hand on our lives, because that is the only way we can deal with our stubborn sins and the habits of a lifetime. Some of us have struggled for twenty years with an awful temper; some constantly fight a compulsion to exaggerate or lie; some wrestle with immoral thoughts. In the end we accept these things as unchangeable parts of our personality. But as we saw in Chapter 4, God is unchanging, and because of that he has the power to change us. But first we have to recognise that we need to change, that our hearts are not centred on God as they should be.

## Openness

However, recognising that God wants to work in us is not the same as allowing him to do so. If I am ill I may know that an antibiotic will make me feel better, but that is quite different from taking the time and trouble to visit the doctor and get a prescription.

This second stage requires action on our part. We may recognise the symptoms, but we need to be open enough to allow God to reach into our lives and cure us. Sometimes the cure is instantaneous — as if God snaps his fingers and it happens — and sometimes it is slow. Silt-like layers of pain may have built up in us, and God works gently, removing them one by one. The main thing is that we should be open to receive God's healing touch, however it comes.

## Ministry and prayer

Sometimes we need the help of other people in order to open our hearts. Many of us are so prone to self-deception that we can even fool ourselves, though we may have a lurking suspicion that underneath everything we are spiritually bankrupt. To fill that emptiness we need prayer, and we would rather do it alone. After all, who wants to admit to the rest of the church that their heart is not right with God, when they have spent the last few years polishing their image?

Yet in Scripture many of the prayers happen in a corporate context: 'For where two or three come together in my name, there am I with them' (Mt 18:20). Faith is built up by other people, and it is strengthened by being part of the people of God. The house group, or the worship service, or the prayer partnership can be a powerful channel for the Holy Spirit to reach us and work in us.

*A matter of will*

In the end, though, the business of reordering our private world is a matter of the will. It requires a decision to act, and the faith to believe that God is ready to come to us. If that decision is made in a moment of emotion, it will last for a week or a month and then fade. What we need is an act of will, in conjunction with the Spirit, to sustain the effort when we don't feel like praying, or can't be bothered to concentrate, or when the call of the old habits and sins is very strong. Being open to God can be very frightening, not least because it makes us face up to our true selves, and we may not like what we see. That is when we need to be strong in our will to do the will of God, day after day.

If we can do so, we will be rewarded a thousand times over, for the heart which is truly centred on God has peace and power and love. We will no longer be merely going through the motions of the Christian life, but fulfilling all the glorious possibilities of God's will for us. In the name of Jesus and in the power of the Holy Spirit, we will be part of God's positive kingdom, working for the coming of that kingdom over the whole earth.

**Kingsway Publications**

Kingsway Publications publishes books to encourage spiritual values in the home, church and society. The list includes Bibles, popular paperbacks, more specialist volumes, booklets, and a range of children's fiction.

Kingsway Publications is owned by The Servant Trust, a Christian charity run by representatives of the evangelical church in Britain, committed to serving God in publishing and music.

For further information on the Trust, including details of how you may be able to support its work, please write to:

The Secretary
The Servant Trust
1 St Anne's Road
Eastbourne
East Sussex  BN21 3UN
England